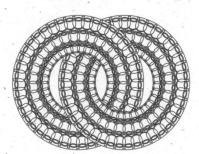

Truth Has a Different Shape

TRUTH HAS A DIFFERENT SHAPE

KARI L. O'DRISCOLL

CAVANKERRY PRESS

CavanKerry Press Ltd.
Fort Lee, New Jersey
www.cavankerrypress.org

Publisher's Cataloging-In-Publication Data
(Prepared by The Donohue Group, Inc.)
Names: O'Driscoll, Kari, author.
Title: Truth has a different shape / Kari L. O'Driscoll.
Description: First edition. | Fort Lee, New Jersey : CavanKerry Press Ltd., 2020.
Identifiers: ISBN 9781933880761 | ISBN 9781933880778 (ebook)
Subjects: LCSH: O'Driscoll, Kari—Family. | Mothers—Biography. | Motherhood—
    Psychological aspects. | Caregivers—Psychology. | Self-sacrifice—Prevention. |
    LCGFT: Autobiographies.
Classification: LCC HQ759 .O37 2020 (print) | LCC HQ759 (ebook) | DDC
    306.8743092—dc23

Cover and interior text design by Ryan Scheife, Mayfly Design
First Edition 2020, Printed in the United States of America

CavanKerry Press is grateful for the support it receives from the New Jersey State Council on the Arts.

Also by Kari O'Driscoll

*One Teenager at a Time: Developing Self-Awareness
and Critical Thinking in Adolescents*
(2019)

For Cameron, wherever you may be

Spiral galaxies are composed of three component parts, known as the bulge, the spiral, and the halo. The bulge is the central disc where there is a high concentration of stars, dust, and gas. The spiral arms pinwheel out from the bulge to form new stars and burn brighter than the bulge. The halo is the glow of older stars and dark matter that reaches far out in to the galaxy.

Contents

Prologue: 2011

I am a great mom. I love being a mom. And the thought of taking care of my mom fills me with rage. It's complicated.

In August, Mom came to visit for a week, and I learned that, even though she now has grandchildren—my daughters—a week is too long. My girls are old enough now that they spend much of their free time lying on beanbags, ear buds blasting pop music, or sprawled across their beds with a book. When they do venture out of their bedrooms, it is to forage in the pantry or stand in front of the refrigerator letting all the cold air out. All of this leaves me to entertain my mother alone.

I am uncomfortable with peopled silence. I can sit alone in silence for hours, writing, meditating, reading, but when others are around, I feel compelled to make conversation. When I am with Mom, I talk for all the years I felt that she wasn't the mother I needed her to be. I talk to prove how well I turned out in spite of her. I talk for the hours she spent in her dark bedroom trying to shut out the life she was in, and for the times she stood in the kitchen, artificially cheerful, pretending that the life we were living was somehow normal.

It is in my nature to shed light on the elephant in the room, throw open the shades, and talk, but I've learned do it in a roundabout way. After years of getting in trouble for being direct, I've discovered a different method. I talk about my life now, giving examples of how I am present in my girls' lives, mentally patting myself on the back. I talk to prove to Mom that I am a better mother to my daughters than I was to my sister. I talk to prove to Mom that I am a better mother to my daughters than she was to me. I know I am being mean and petty, and incredibly passive-aggressive, but I still feel justified. Even so, it's not as satisfying as I want it to be.

By the second day of Mom's visit, I realize something is wrong.

"Have you guys watched *The Amazing Race* this season? We are so disgusted with the way they treat each other this time around."

I have answered this question three times today. At the dinner table, she confuses details, repeats herself, can't keep track of the conversation. I wrestle with my own thoughts: *Is she tired? Not paying attention because we aren't important enough for her to track the conversation? Is she losing it? Is this how Alzheimer's starts?*

By the third day, I find myself getting short with her. I can't look at her face, so I schedule outings to local tourist attractions even though I know it will wear her out. I have to keep moving, keep her out of the house, keep her from reminding me that she is losing her mind.

The day she leaves, I come home and cry deep, ugly sobs face down on my comforter. Glistening snot streaks criss-cross the pillow shams, and damp spots make eye marks on the bed.

Why am I so angry with her?

The answer comes loud and clear, a fire alarm in the night.

She's gonna get off the hook. And I'm going to end up taking care of her.

I alternate between worrying that Mom will forget the things I most want to know and wondering at the irony of it all. If she were starting to descend into Alzheimer's, it would be the perfect way for her to get away with not ever giving me the answers I want.

For weeks, I am shaken. I poll my siblings and hers to see if anyone else has noticed her memory loss and odd behavior. My sister Katy seems slightly concerned but Chris, the oldest, makes excuses.

"She might be on some new diabetes medication that is affecting her memory. I know she's been pretty stressed out lately, so that's probably it."

"Dude. That's not it. I had to remind her three times what time the train was coming. She still can't remember what hotel she's staying in for Terri's wedding, and Jan has emailed her twice with the details. That seems odd to me."

"I dunno. What do you want me to do?" Even though we are talking on the phone, I can picture his innocent shrug clearly.

Why am I always the one who points out the steaming pile of shit on the front lawn while everyone else looks up at the sky or wanders off? I notice it, I get to clean it up. That's the way it works. *Finders keepers. The one who smelt it, dealt it.*

I fantasize about pulling one of Mom's signature moves and pretending not to notice. She lives four hours away from me and she doesn't seem worried. What if I just leave it alone? What if, in some poetic twist, as she loses her memories, she loses her filter, too, and tells me the things I've always wanted to know? That thought makes me laugh out loud until I consider the opposite. *What if she dies and her memories die with her? What if I never get to the truth? What if she never has to admit that she left all of us hanging for years?*

I begin to wonder about memory, especially as I talk to Katy and Chris about the things that happened when we were kids. Even if Chris and I were in the same room at the same time, we recall different details and assign different levels of importance to things that happened. I remember things that my siblings have no inkling of, and sometimes it makes me think I'm crazy.

Did we all get the same coloring page, characters and places outlined in thick black ink, and just fill them in differently? Did Katy's mind scribble and scratch holes in the paper or color inside the lines while I set some of the pages aside for later? There are so many holes in my memory that I hold on tightly to the things I do recall. I've filled certain pages in with Technicolor clarity and framed them on the wall of my mind. They are among my most prized possessions. But are they real? Are they True?

Sometimes I think Truth is like a rubber band. We stretch it with the telling and retelling, emphasizing certain details and ignoring others to make it a coherent story. Human beings have a love affair with good stories. I read somewhere that our brains release dopamine every time we hear one that makes sense, whose pieces all fit together neatly, even if the ultimate picture isn't a pretty one. We like loose ends tied up and the players all accounted for, but as we tell and retell our stories, we can stretch that rubber band to the point where the Truth is a different shape altogether than where it started.

For good or for bad, those memories, my Truth, have shaped the person I've become and if I don't hang on to them, I might lose myself. Here is the story of what I know.

Book One:

The Bulge

1975-1991

Building a Family

A few months before the end of the Vietnam War, an airplane filled with hundreds of orphaned children took off from Saigon. There wasn't much time to get out before the bombing started, so the plane was stuffed with children tucked in two to a seat and the rest were strapped to the floor in the cargo area. Shortly after takeoff, there was an explosion and the C-58 Galaxy was forced to try landing in a rice paddy, but it hit a dike and burst into flames, killing seventy-eight children and fifty adults on board. More than 150 others survived, were loaded onto another airplane, and were evacuated to the United States to be adopted. My sister, not quite two months old at the time, was one of those who lay strapped to the floor of the second airplane for the long flight to the United States.

I am three years old and incredibly excited to be a big sister. The day they bring a little baby with a shock of corn silk hair to our house in Medford, Oregon, there are lots of strangers with cameras hanging around. They take pictures of Mommy and Daddy and Chris, and a few of me sitting in the rocking chair in the living room with the new baby wrapped up in my lap. I love the attention, especially because Mommy dressed me up in my church clothes today.

I look straight at one of the cameras and announce, "I love this baby. She is mine and I will always take care of her."

Everyone laughs and I grin as big as I can and give that tiny little baby a kiss on her forehead. She is so cute! Just like my very own doll. I have a boy baby doll named David, but he just has a plastic head with no hair and he isn't warm and soft like this little girl.

We got this new baby because I ruined Mommy for having babies. She says she had to stay on the couch all day long when she was pregnant with me and her doctor said no more. She already had my older brother, Chris, but she wanted a house full of babies, so she was sad that she couldn't have any more. But one of Daddy's friends from the war called and asked if we wanted one of these babies and Mommy said "yes, yes, yes, this must be God's work!"

Her name is Katy and she is so tiny—Mommy says only about six pounds. She is sick a lot. She is always throwing up and has really stinky diapers and for a while, she goes to the hospital because she has a worm in her tummy. When she comes home, she starts getting chubby and she sleeps a lot more. I love holding her and playing with her thin, black hair that sticks straight up all over her head. I put my hand on it to hold it down and when I let go, it sproings right back up again.

When I am five and Katy is two and Chris is eight years old, we move to a new town for Daddy's work. Our house in Klamath Falls is huge with lots of steps and there are so many kids in our neighborhood. Katy and I share a bedroom at the very tip-top of the house. It is really big with a huge closet, and Daddy builds us a wooden kitchen to put in there so we can play house and not have our toys in his way. Mommy says we get to decorate our room any way we want, and we choose yellow Holly Hobbie bedspreads and pillows and I let Katy have the bed farthest from the door so I can protect her in case someone comes in. When our beds are made, they look like twins and so do we most of the time because Mommy makes our clothes from the same fabric. I like it that way because I can always find Katy if I just look down to see what I'm wearing.

Chris has a bedroom right across the hall from us with bunk beds and a neat desk up against the window. I'm glad he's up here, too, because Mommy and Daddy's bedroom is all the way in the basement, which is really far away if we need something. Daddy likes it down there because it's quieter. He says we kids can get really obnoxious sometimes.

I don't really understand what Daddy does for work, but I like seeing him all dressed up in his suit every day. I sit on the edge of his bed and watch him swirl that long silky piece of fabric around and tuck it in, and it seems like magic because it's always neat and tidy when he's done.

Sometimes he lets me sit on his lap and touch the pins he wears for Rotary and Kiwanis Club, but I really want to take off his big Marine Corps ring with the giant red stone in it and put it on my finger. He never takes it off, though, even when he washes and waxes the cars or mows the lawn. But it is always sparkly and clean. Every Sunday Daddy gets out his shoe-shining kit and polishes his shoes with a *brshhh-brshhh*, swiping a soft brush back and forth until they are perfect. Daddy likes it like that. He says they taught him how to keep things clean and neat in the Marines and it's important.

We have to keep things clean, too, and he tries to make it fun. He taught Chris and me how to make hospital corners on our beds and tries to bounce a quarter off of them like they did in boot camp. I'm pretty good but Katy is too little to pay attention and do it right so Daddy gets frustrated with her a lot. I think I should just do it for her and tell him she did it so he won't get angry anymore. It's not her fault she's so little.

We learn all about how to be neat and tidy at the table, too. Daddy says napkin in your lap, sit up straight, elbows off the table, and never talk with food in your mouth. Stay at the table until your plate is clean and ask to be excused when you're done. Katy sometimes doesn't clean her plate and has to sit there for a long time after dinner by herself. She is so stubborn! I used to help her with food when Daddy and Mommy weren't looking, but I got caught and now I have to sit on the other side of the table for a while. Daddy says he isn't paying good money for food that goes to waste, but I just think her tummy is too small to eat all the food he piles on her plate.

Chris and I go to Roosevelt Elementary School, which is close to our house. We just walk down the front steps, across the street, through the alley, and it's right there. It's a big brick building with lots of steps. I go downstairs to kindergarten and he goes upstairs to fourth grade with mean old Mrs. Tacchini. I have Mrs. Ludwig, who is older than dirt and the only kindergarten teacher this school has ever had. She is nice, though, and she likes me. Katy stays home with Mommy to play and Daddy goes to work. Sometimes I see Chris on the playground at recess and he waves at me and that makes me happy. This school is much bigger than our old Montessori school in Medford where Chris and I were in the same classroom, so it's nice to spot his curly red hair and freckly smile all the way across the field some days.

———

I am standing in the corner of the living room, but nobody is paying attention to me. The whole room is full of Katy's screams because she is in big trouble. Mom takes the wooden spoon out of the crock on the counter and Katy's hands are shoved way down in the back of her pants. She is trying to cover her bottom so it won't hurt so bad and she keeps running in circles—her little legs moving fast like someone in a cartoon—even though Mommy isn't chasing her. She is just standing in the doorway with the spoon in her hand and a big frown on her face. Her face is all red and I can't tell if she wants to yell or cry.

Katy keeps yelling, "NO NO NONONONONONONONO," over and over again and it scares me. It sounds like she is really hurt, like broken bones or bleeding or something but she isn't. Mommy didn't even hit her yet.

I step out of the shadowy corner and tell Mommy, "I did it. Spank me. It was my fault. She didn't do anything. She's too young. I'm the one who made her do it. Spank me. Please. Please. Spank me." I start crying and I think it convinces Mommy that I really did do it, but I'm not crying because I'm guilty. I'm crying because I'm sad and afraid and I don't want Katy to get hurt.

There are two things I want more than anything—to be taken care of and to take care of Katy—but Daddy says I'm a big girl and that means taking care of myself most of the time. That means when I get that sad little spot in my tummy that makes me want to cuddle up in someone's arms and act like a baby, I'm ashamed. But I can mostly squash that awful feeling by cuddling Katy. Taking care of her makes her feel better too, so snuggling with her is magic for both of us. I'm really glad she lets me, but sometimes Mommy gets upset that Katy wants me when she is sad. It's kind of funny because I would go to Mommy for a cuddle if I could, but I can't because she agrees with Daddy that I'm a big girl.

———

Things are so exciting around here right now! We are getting a new brother. Mommy says he is coming from the Philippine Islands and she showed me on a map where that is. She says our numbers will be even now, two boys and two girls, and the best part is that he's not a baby. He's a kid my age! He's almost eight and he should be in third grade with me, but being in an orphanage means he's behind, so he's gonna start in second grade. Mommy and Dad named him Cameron Alexander and decided his new birthday is February 28, the day he will come live with us.

We set up a little party and he is so surprised! He is a little taller than me and has long, skinny arms and legs. His skin is milk chocolate like Katy's and he has that same black, black hair, too. When he smiles, which is a lot, the whole day gets brighter. His cheeks squinch up and his white teeth show and it's just like sunshine. His left eye is this cloudy, swamp green color, which is kind of gross, but he doesn't get mad when I ask him about it. Chris and Katy come over to hear the story of how a bunch of boys were playing firefighter and he got jabbed in the eye with a stick someone pretended was a fire hose. I cover my eye with both hands when he says that because it hurts me to think about it.

Mommy made her best lasagna for dinner to celebrate. It takes hours to make and she only does it for special occasions, but this is definitely one special day. I'm so hungry from smelling it by the time we finally sit down at the dinner table, I can't stand it. Mommy and Daddy sit at their ends of the table and the boys sit across from Katy and me. We are allowed to put our elbows on the table to clasp our hands and pray and I sneak peeks at Cameron when I'm supposed to have my eyes shut because I wonder if he knows how to do it. I guess someone at the orphanage taught him to have good table manners, because he's very quiet and polite and Daddy doesn't have to tell him how to behave at all.

We all clean our plates, but nobody does it as well as Cameron. His plate is totally wiped clean! Mommy is a great cook and her lasagna is the best, so it was easy to eat everything, but tonight we ate *everything*. There isn't a speck of food left except for one piece of French bread on Mommy's plate. Cameron keeps sliding his eyes over to look at it but he just sits with his hands in his lap and I can tell he doesn't want to ask for it. I look at Mommy and point to her bread with my eyes and then tip my head to Cam and she smiles and gives it to him and he says thank you a million times. Dad doesn't even correct him for talking with his mouth full.

Mommy says later that she gave him three helpings of lasagna and she is amazed by how much he eats. I wonder if he is just being polite, but after a few days I realize he is really hungry. I guess he didn't get too much to eat at the orphanage, so he must think he's in Heaven here. Daddy warns him that he's going to get fat and when Cam laughs, I glare at Daddy. Cam doesn't realize how mean that is, cuz Daddy says one of the worst things is being fat, but I don't want him making fun of Cameron.

Cameron feels like one of us right away. He is great at hide-and-seek and he loves playing soccer. He sleeps in the bottom bunk in Chris's room and he is always ready to learn a new game. I feel like he's my twin because he isn't little like Katy or bigger and cool like Chris. He is my shadow, Mommy says, and I like that. It's hard not to smile when I'm around him. He seems to live in this little cloud of happiness—like Pigpen in the Snoopy comic strip. Cameron smiles all the time and acts like everything in our house is from outer space. He wanders around the rooms touching things and running his fingertips along the velour couch, grinning like it's Christmas Eve or something. Every time I come anywhere close to him, I get sucked into his happiness cloud and the next thing I know, I'm looking at everything like it's Christmas, too. On his first day of school, we walk through the alley holding hands. I can't wait to introduce him to his teacher and all my friends.

Some of the kids at school are really mean to Cameron, though, and it makes me mad. He looks different because of his cloudy eye and his dark skin, so some of the boys chase him on the playground and call him "wetback" and "beaner," or wave their hands in his face to see if he's blind. He is really fast, so they mostly don't catch him, but when we have recess at the same time, I go yell at them and tell them to knock it off. Chris goes to Ponderosa Junior High now, so he isn't there to help me, but my girlfriend Delia's dad is a lawyer and he taught her how to argue better than anyone, and she sometimes yells at the mean boys with me. The teachers mostly say to let them all play and get it out of their system, but that's the only time Cam doesn't smile and it makes me sad.

I wonder if they'll be mean to Katy when she comes to school here. She looks a lot like Cam with her jet-black hair and brown skin. I never thought about that before, but now I'm worried. She's so tiny and she's a girl. I hope the boys don't tease her like that.

Cameron starts playing on Chris's soccer team and makes some friends that way because he's so good. Even though Chris is two years older than him, Daddy is the coach and he lets Cameron play. Cam is so happy on the soccer field and it's the only time we aren't together. Chris likes having him on the team, but sometimes Daddy yells at him to play more like Cameron and Chris's face gets really dark red.

Collapse

Katy is excited to start school and isn't afraid of Mrs. Ludwig at all, even though she is so old she can't stand up straight and her face has more wrinkles than skin. She wears her hair piled up on top of her head and always has a skirt and sweater on with her glasses dangling from a sparkly chain. When she leans out to say hello, they swing away from her and you think they're gonna smack you in the forehead.

I walk Katy to her classroom and help her put her stuff away before walking to the far end of the hall to wave at Cameron in his classroom. He grins back at me and I know he's gonna be okay. His teacher is really nice. I head upstairs to my classroom and wonder if this year will be hard. Mostly, though, I'm glad to be back at school. Mommy and Daddy are fighting all the time. Not in front of us, but there's always yelling and I can tell when Mommy has been crying. Katy is also getting spanked a lot, even when I try to get in the middle and stop it. She can't control herself when she gets mad, so she screams and throws stuff and sometimes breaks things or hurts herself. She's also a biter, but I never tell when she bites me because I know she'll get spanked again and I hate that.

This summer, I tried to stay outside with Cameron and Chris, shooting baskets or playing capture the flag with the neighbor kids or helping Katy find a good spot for hide-and-seek. Maybe now that we're back in school, things will be better for everyone.

Saturday at breakfast, Daddy looks at the boys and says it is a good day to wash and wax the cars and I ask if I can help. I don't want to get stuck inside doing dishes or playing house with Katy. I'd rather be outside.

Plus, Mommy says she's gonna work in the yard today and I hate weeding. Hanging out with the boys sounds way more fun.

Daddy doesn't look excited. I know he thinks I shouldn't be doing boy things like mowing the lawn or playing soccer, but I'm stubborn. I wait quietly with my hands in my lap and Mommy doesn't say a word or even look at him, so he finally says I can.

"Daddy's girl!" Chris pushes me hard as soon as we clean the table and head upstairs to get dressed. "You're such a brownnoser! God! Always sucking up to Dad. Why can't you just go play with some dolls or plant flowers with Mom? Leave us boys to do the man stuff."

I turn around and push him back, and he tackles me and sits on me and starts tickling me, which is the thing I hate most in the world. It makes me feel like I'm trapped and I'm going to die and I get all panicky and breathe funny and he just laughs. Cameron is frozen like he can't tell if I am okay or not because I am laughing, which is what you do when you're being tickled, even if you don't want to, so pretty soon I start screaming. There isn't much screaming because I can't really breathe, but it is enough to get Cam to go run for Daddy.

When Daddy comes in, he yells, "What the hell is going on? Jesus! You kids!"

Chris jumps up and shrugs at Daddy all innocent. "I don't know. I was just teasing her. She's such a baby, I swear! Why does she have to come and help us do the cars today? She can't even take a joke!"

But it wasn't a joke. I saw the look on his face. He was mad when he was on me. He wasn't being funny, no matter what he says. Now that I can breathe, I start crying and Daddy shakes his head.

"Take it easy, Kari. Don't be so dramatic, huh? He was just messing around. Go get dressed before I change my mind about letting you help. And, boys? Why don't you two mow and edge the lawn together, instead? We can get it all done today if we divide and conquer."

Daddy just made it worse. Chris is right—I am the "Daddy's girl." Now he is going to have to work with Cam by himself while I get to be with Daddy alone. I am scared and happy. Chris isn't going to forget this and Daddy will make sure I do a perfect, Perfect Job *or else*. But at least I don't have to pull weeds or play house.

The thing Daddy hates most of all is people who are incompetent. He says those are people who can't get things done and Keep Order. He is really good at both of those things. He knows lots of details and pays attention to everything and it makes him crazy when there is chaos. He has schedules for washing and waxing the cars, taking care of the lawn, and paying the bills. Whenever he comes home and there is a big mess or a lot of crying and fighting, he gets pretty mad. I think crying is worst of all because he wants us to be tough and crying means you are weak. So does being fat or lazy. Weak is a sin, Daddy says.

"Crying is a waste of time, Kari. Remember that. The important thing is to never let 'em see you sweat. If Chris knows he's bugging you, he will just keep doing it. If you ignore him, he'll stop. And if you cry, he wins. Don't make a big deal out of stuff like that."

He shows me how to dip the soft mitt into the wax to get just a little bit and swirl it on to the car like lotion. This lotion doesn't sink in; it dries white in the sunshine. When it's dry, we take a clean rag and rub in the same swirly motion to wipe it off and the car shines like brand new. I forget to listen to Daddy because I am busy trying to figure out why the rag gets all black and smudgy even though the wax is white. I love, love, love the way the car looks after. It's so easy to tell which parts we did and which ones we missed, so I know I can do a Perfect Job as long as I Pay Attention.

He pokes me and raises his eyebrows.

"Okay, Daddy. I'm sorry. I just hate being tickled and I know he said he was playing, but I think he was being mean and trying to hurt me."

"That's what boys do, Kar. You have to learn to toughen up and not let him hurt you. It's just a game. And sometimes, when we play games, we do get hurt, but you just get up and keep on going."

I want to tell Daddy that everything I saw in Chris's eyes when he pinned my arms to the floor with his knees and pounded his knuckle into my chest told me he wanted to hurt me, that he was angry. I want to say that that wasn't any kind of play I understood—that was rage. His frozen, angry face scared me more than the bruises on my ribs and the feeling of being trapped. Why would my big brother want to hurt me for real? I don't understand. But I see Daddy wrestling with Chris and Cameron like that sometimes, too, and Daddy always calls it a game, even when he has that same angry look in his eyes.

————————

Today, Cameron stayed home sick and I'm surprised. He is almost never sick and he loves school so much. It feels weird to walk to school without him, but Katy and I go together, holding hands through the alley, and I walk her to her class like always before heading to my classroom. She sometimes doesn't want me to leave and I hate leaving, too. The kindergarten classroom's the cheeriest room in the whole school with lots of art and small, round tables with boxes of scissors and crayons in the middle. But I'm a good kid, so I kiss her on the top of her head, remind her that Mom is coming to get her at lunchtime, and trek upstairs to my classroom with its rows of desks facing the chalkboard.

Walking home by myself feels odd, but at least it isn't far. I hope Cam is feeling good enough to play outside after school because it's warm outside. When I get to the end of the alley, I can see our big yellow house down the block on the other side of the street and there's a white van in the driveway with the engine chugging. If I squint, I can see it says Holt Adoption Services on it and my heart leaps. Are we getting another brother or sister today? Is that why Cam stayed home? To help welcome the new kid? I stop to look for cars before I cross the street and I see the front door open. Cameron is standing there with a suitcase in his hand, just looking at his feet. A lady comes up the steps and puts her hand on his back to lead him to the van, and before I can get across the street and down the block, he is inside and the van is backing out of the driveway. I run up the front steps to holler at Mom, but change my mind and look back at Cam in the van.

I stop at the top of the porch and turn around, holding my breath, my hand on the black iron railing. Cameron looks out the window at me, one of his hands on the glass, and I think he feels like I do—confused and stuck and drowning. I look at him like I'm looking in a mirror, my mouth open and my eyes huge. The smoke from the back of the van curls up past his window and the van drives down the steep hill away from our house. There's a thick ball in my throat and I sit down hard, my backpack thumping behind me. The front door is still open but nobody is there. I sit there for a long time until I hear Mommy calling me from the kitchen to come in and shut the door.

I walk slowly up the stairs to the top floor and peek in the boys' bedroom. Chris isn't home from school yet. Cam's bed is made just like always, but his dresser drawers are empty and his soccer ball isn't there. He isn't sick. He is gone.

––––––––––

"Can I write him letters?" My voice is whiny and shaky.

Mom shakes her head and Daddy won't look up from his dinner.

I don't understand. Chris shrugs his shoulders like he does all the time these days and Katy just sits quietly. Mom's lips are in a thin line. She won't talk.

After dinner, I ask to be excused and instead of going outside to play, I go upstairs and sit on my bed to think. Daddy didn't like Cameron as much as he should have. He was always making fun of Cameron and now Cameron's gone. Daddy was always pushing Chris to be tougher, especially in soccer, saying things like, "You need to work harder. You're just lazy! For God's sake, you're the coach's son and this little kid is better than you!" Daddy is always yelling at Katy, too, and calling us both crybabies. When Katy comes up to play house, I tell her we better all be really good from now on. No being weak or lazy or making a mess. We have to Keep Order.

––––––––––

I am really good at math and counting things. I know that there are sixteen steps from the top of the house to the main floor and fourteen more down to the basement. And that's good, because after Cameron is taken away, Mom and Daddy say I started sleepwalking to their bedroom every night. I don't remember any of it except sometimes I wake up when Daddy is carrying me back upstairs to my bedroom in the dark. He says I scare him half to death, showing up at the end of their bed and just standing there silently every night. I figure the only way I can do it without breaking my neck is I must be counting the steps in my sleep.

The craziest thing is that nobody will talk about Cameron. All the pictures of him are gone and even his bike isn't in the garage anymore. The first night after he was taken, Mom asked me to set the table and when I counted out six knives, she reached over and took one out of my hand and put it back.

"That's not right, Kari. That's too many."

How does a person just disappear and nobody talks about it?

––––––––––

One day, Katy puts on her Wonder Woman Underoos and refuses to take them off. Every time I see her getting dressed, I hear the jingle in my head: *Underoos. The underwear that's fun to wear.*

She's still wearing them a few days later when Mom begs her to take them off. She stinks like little kid sweat and pee and finally, Mom convinces Katy to let her wash them while the two of us take a bath, but we get done too fast and they aren't dry yet, so Katy throws a fit. She's pulling her hair and shrieking and flinging herself around on the floor. It's a good thing Daddy isn't here or he'd spank her silly. Mom tries to wrap her in a bath towel and I run around the corner and snatch the Underoos out of the dryer. I dash back to the bathroom and turn the hair dryer on full blast and Katy finally stops screaming when I point the air so it puffs the underwear bottoms out like a balloon. She rolls over and sits up cross-legged on the floor to watch, tears skidding down her cheeks. When they are dry enough to wear, I hold them out to her and she hugs me, taking those big, choppy breaths you have to take when you cry really hard. It feels good to wrap my arms around her warm little body and I'm happy I made her happy. After that, she won't take them off no matter what Mom says.

A few days later, we drag our Moon Boots and heavy jackets on before walking to school because it snowed a lot. Chris catches the bus at the bottom of the hill, so he gets to slide all the way down to the stop, but Katy and I have to tromp through the alley. The best part is that nobody has driven through it yet, so we can make our own fresh tracks.

"Have a good day, girls!" Mom stands on the front porch and watches us crunch through the snow and look both ways before crossing the street.

I take Katy's hand and Mom goes back inside, but halfway down the alley, Katy pulls her glove free from mine and swings her backpack off her shoulder.

"What are you doing? We're gonna be late." I want to get to school early enough to see if there's a snowball fight on the playground. Katy doesn't answer, but bends over her pack and unzips it, her silky black hair falling forward to cover her face. She takes off her jacket and stuffs the puffy mass inside and then kicks the heels of her boots against the ground to loosen and slip them off.

"What are you doing?!" I shriek. "You're going to freeze to death!"

She peeks up at me beneath a curtain of hair and grins as she pops the snap on her corduroy pants. She sheds the rest of her clothes and slowly transforms into Wonder Woman right there in the alley. I force her boots back onto her feet and drag her jacket out of the pack to wrap around her. She is too big for me to carry, but at least I can try to keep her warm. She's only letting me because I'm not trying to put her clothes back on.

I stuff her pants and sweater inside her backpack and swing it over my shoulder with mine. She is grinning like a fool. Her black hair shines in the sunlight and she stands up straight and tall. The teachers are gonna think we're crazy, but I don't care. This morning, she is Wonder Woman.

Daddy calls a family meeting in the living room and, at first, Chris and I fight over the round chair because it's the best. It is covered in soft, gold fabric and you can make it go in circles if you wiggle your butt just right. We can never keep track of who got it last, so we bicker about whose turn it is, but Daddy gets mad and tells us to knock it off. I let Chris have it and go to the couch to sit next to Katy. Daddy sits on the other end of the couch, but only on the very edge, like he's gonna get up and leave any second, and Mom stands in the doorway to the dining room. Her eyes are all red from crying and, even though that happens a lot, I suddenly don't want to be there.

"Kids, your mother and I are not going to be married anymore. I'm going to go stay at the El Dorado Hotel over by the Hasty Freez and you can come visit me anytime you want to."

Mom's face is like a statue and Chris looks mad. Katy tangles her fingers in her hair and twirls it around and around and then sticks her fingers and her hair in her mouth and starts sucking. I have a million questions but the only one I think is safe to ask is if he would take us for soft serve if we come visit. It's a stupid question, but it won't get me in trouble, so I ask. He laughs.

"Sure, Squirt. It's only a block away."

I start having lots of nightmares after Daddy moves out, but I don't ever sleepwalk into Mom's room again, I don't think. First Cameron and then Daddy. My family is getting slowly shot to bits, one by one, like when we play Asteroids on the Atari. I start to wonder who is next and then I realize it isn't enough to be good and Keep Order anymore. I have to try to keep the rest of us together now.

I decide that maybe writing Daddy letters will let him know how important it is for him to come back home to be with us, so I write him one every week.

December 4, 1980

Dear Daddy,

I love and miss you very much. You are the greatest thing that has happened to me ever since I was born (obviously!). Tonight I was thinking about you and I felt how lonely you must be. I love you!!!!!! It just isn't right without you here. I miss you!!!!!!!!!!!

Love ya,
Kari

Every time we see him, he hugs me extra tight and says thank you for the letters. But he never writes back and he doesn't move back in with us, either.

———

Mom has to get a job to put food on the table after Daddy leaves. She goes to work in a bank so she can be home on the weekends, but that means Chris and I have to pack our own lunches—and Katy's too—and

Katy has to go to a babysitter's house after morning kindergarten. Sometimes, when Chris has after-school practices, I join Katy at Jan's house until someone comes to get us.

Jan lives right across the street from our school and she has three kids, Clayton, Shawna, and Stevie. She is divorced, too, so her job is to take care of kids in her house all day long. I wonder why Mom didn't choose that job because she loves kids so much.

We get to see Daddy on Sunday mornings because we stop going to church after the divorce. Daddy takes us hiking when it's sunny and warm and he says that this can be our church now. I miss the kids at Sunday School and the classes Chris and I took for catechism and First Communion and one morning before we go to Daddy's, I ask Mom if she is going to church without us.

"No, Kari, I don't go anymore. That church doesn't let you back if you get divorced. It's a sin. When you get married in the Catholic Church, you have to stay together forever, no matter how awful things get, and since your father left, we can't go back." Her voice is all quivery and she has tears in her eyes and I feel bad for asking.

I ask Chris what he thinks when we are alone in Daddy's living room. Daddy and Katy are in the kitchen making eggs and bacon for breakfast.

Chris shrugs. "I don't care. Gives me more time to sleep and I hated going to classes every week, anyway."

I can't help but think that we are getting punished for something we didn't do. Mom and Daddy sinned, not us. Why are we getting kicked out of the church? We already lost a brother and we're kind of losing Daddy. Now we have to lose our church, too?

Managing

"Mom, that's not how you're supposed to do it. Here, I'll show you." She is making sandwiches for us to take to the park, but Katy doesn't like mayonnaise on hers. She only likes two thin pieces of turkey and one slice of cheese and nothing else. I get up from the breakfast bar and walk to where she has everything set up—the loaf of bread and Frito-Lay multipack box so we can each choose our favorite flavor.

"You are just like your father. Everything so precise."

But she hates Daddy now. So, if I'm just like him ... I get a heavy feeling in the pit of my stomach and I want to run out of the room, but if I don't make Katy's sandwich the way she likes it, she won't eat and the picnic will be ruined. I duck my head and pull two slices of bread from the package in front of me.

As I spread the mayonnaise on my own sandwich, I fight to keep the tears from spilling out by tipping my head back as far as I can. Mom hates Daddy and I'm just like him. I'm not trying to be like Daddy, I'm just trying to make things better. If Mom is the first one up in the morning, her coffee cup should be the one closest to the front of the cupboard. That's what I think when I empty the dishwasher. If Chris likes Lucky Charms better than Cap'n Crunch, the box should be out on the counter the night before so he can grab it and pour without having to rummage around in the pantry. When Daddy lived here, I knew he didn't like me to roll his socks because it stretches them and they fall down, so I just folded them in a pair when I did the laundry. But Mom likes hers rolled because they fit in the drawer better, so I'm sure to alternate which sock I roll on the outside so they stretch evenly.

One morning, someone comes in to my classroom from the office and pulls my teacher aside. The class is quiet and we watch as the teacher's eyes get big and then her mouth and forehead get all pinched up. She waves her hand and turns back to the blackboard and the office lady walks to my desk. My heart pounds like crazy. Something bad has happened. Is it Katy? Chris?

"We need you in Mrs. Ludwig's classroom for a minute, Kari."

I'm so confused.

She explains that Katy is throwing one of her tantrums and they can't get ahold of Mommy so I have to come help.

When I get downstairs, the classroom is a disaster. There are chairs lying on the floor and pens scattered all over. Katy is inside the kindergarten teepee wailing and another kid is sitting on the reading circle rug crying hysterically as Mrs. Ludwig comforts him, even though she's too old to bend all the way down anymore. I stand in the doorway for a minute and when she sees me, she nods her head toward the teepee.

"Katy bit Timmy and then she started throwing things and knocking the chairs over. I sent the other children out to play with my aide because they were scared, but I can't get Katy to come out. I'm afraid she is going to hurt someone else or herself. Could you please talk to her? I'm sure she would be happy to see you."

I am so embarrassed. I can't believe she did this here. She gets pretty crazy mad at home sometimes and she is a biter, but I never thought she would do this at school. She knows we're supposed to be good. I nod my head up and down and rush over to poke my head into the teepee. As the flap moves, she starts to yell until she sees it's me and then she curls into a ball on the floor and sobs. I crawl all the way in and wrap my body over hers like a blanket and we rock back and forth until she stops shaking.

After that, I get called to her classroom any time she gets in trouble. It seems like I'm the only one that can get her to calm down and my teacher is mad that I'm missing so much time in class, but Mom can't leave work and Katy is only there for a half day, anyway.

Some days when I go to Jan's, Katy is sitting in front of the TV just staring and doesn't even notice when I come in. I don't blame her. I hate it there. Jan and her kids are all mean, but we have to stay there until Chris gets home.

The best days are when Chris comes home right after school. Those days, I get to pick Katy up from Jan's and go straight home and use the key Mom gave me to keep on a yellow piece of yarn around my neck. I let us in and a few minutes later, Chris is there. Most of the time, when Katy and I get home all she wants to do is curl up with her head in my lap on the couch and read stories until she falls asleep. I don't know why she doesn't take naps at Jan's. She's always so tired. And once, she takes the yarn from around my neck and seesaws it back and forth across her nose while I'm reading. By the time I'm done with the first book, there is a huge split in her nose and she's bleeding all over the place. She rubbed that yarn across her nose so hard, it cut her open but when I ask her if it hurts, she just shrugs her little shoulders. I race her to the bathroom to clean up and find a Band-Aid that will fit across it. There's an orange stain on my yarn necklace now, but at least she didn't get blood on the couch.

By the time I get her cleaned up and back on the couch, it doesn't even take a second story for her to fall asleep. Chris comes downstairs, pokes his head in the living room, and wags his finger for me to follow him. I slide Katy's head off my lap and walk in to the kitchen just as he shoves a barstool over to the fridge to reach up into the cupboard above it.

"What are you doing? There's nothing up there but camping stuff."

He grins at me and I know this is going to be good. He's a little nuts sometimes, but he's pretty smart.

"No shit, Sherlock." He leaps off the stool cradling a package of marsh-mallows and some Hershey's bars. "Grab the graham crackers, dope."

I really hope he's not going to start a fire. Instead, he flings the micro-wave door open.

"What the heck are you doing?"

"Chocolate won't melt unless the marshmallow is warm." He rips open the Jet Puffed package and grins at me with that crazy face he gets sometimes. I freeze and watch as he sets a marshmallow inside and closes the door. A second later he snaps his fingers and grabs a plate to put un-derneath it. He cranks the dial and pushes Start.

"Whoa! Get over here! You gotta see this! Radical!" He waves me over and I run to peek in the window. We stand with our heads together and watch the marshmallow grow and puff up like an air mattress.

"Stop it!" I yell.

He jerks the door open and the marshmallow deflates almost instantly. I hand him a square of graham cracker and he breaks off two rectangles of chocolate, puts them on top and reaches for the marshmallow.

"Shit!" It's too hot and he yelps as he tosses it on to the chocolate, tops it with another graham cracker, and squishes the whole thing down.

"Man, that was cool. And you shouldn't swear."

We make half a dozen s'mores and eat them standing in front of the microwave. My brother is a genius.

Then he goes crazy. He stacks a pyramid of marshmallows on the plate and cranks the microwave on and we watch, mesmerized, as the stack grows into one solid mass. Holding our breath, we see it begin to fill up the microwave and press against the window and when we fling the door open—*PFFFFFFT*—it explodes and stalactites of sugary goo stretch down from the ceiling of the microwave and harden. Chris falls on the floor, holding his sides and shrieking with laughter.

"That was *awesome!* Did you see that explode? Wait til I tell the guys at school!"

My face is burning. What have we done? I grab the spatula from the crock on the counter and start scraping the mess off the inside of the microwave. If Mom finds out, we're dead.

Daddy has a girlfriend. Her name is Susan and she works with Smokey the Bear. I think he thought we would think that was cool, but I don't care. She has a son Chris's age but he is huge—way taller than Chris. He is nice, but I don't like it when we go out with them because they put all of us kids together and just expect us to do stuff like we are all friends, and we aren't. Plus, Daddy and Susan kiss all the time and it makes me mad. What about Mom? She is working hard and she's lonely. I know because I hear her crying at night when I sneak downstairs to get the cat and bring her to our room to sleep.

Susan is so different from Mom. She has two cats and a tiny little house and drives a red sports car. She can't really cook and she talks back to Daddy and she is really nosy.

I don't know what to say to Mom when she asks how our day was. We just got back from hanging out at the park with Daddy and Susan all day and they spoiled us with ice cream and huge bags of chips and I tried really hard not to have fun. Katy can't keep her mouth shut about how great it was and I am shocked when I realize I want to punch her for it. I look at Chris but he just shrugs and heads up to his room to listen to music. I set Katy up with some paper dolls and ask Mom if there's anything I can do.

"It's okay, honey. I'm just going to go to bed early tonight. Make sure Katy brushes her teeth tonight, okay?" She heads downstairs to cry and I wander around the kitchen for a while trying to think of something to do that would be helpful.

———

I hate not having Chris at the same school as us. I feel lonely and frustrated and Katy is still biting kids and having tantrums and I don't know what to do. My teacher is really nice to me, but what I really want is Mom. She's home at night, but she's always tired, and on the weekends, she goes for drives by herself or goes to talk to her pastor at the new church or goes on dates. I wish she would talk to me about what will happen, but the things she says are all about not having enough money and being stressed.

I already know she won't leave work if Katy acts out because she knows I can take care of it, but what if I get sick? She will have to come get me, and maybe we can sit on the couch and sip ginger ale and she will stroke my hair like she used to. There's no way Jan will let me in her house if she thinks I have the stomach flu, so Mom will have to leave work. I feel bad about lying, but one day in class I decide to test it out. I put on a pathetic face and ask to be excused to the bathroom. When I get in there, I lock myself in a stall and make noises like I'm throwing up just in case anyone else is in there. I am too afraid to stick my finger down my throat, but I make my face red and work up a sweat and slowly shuffle back to my classroom and tell my teacher I need to go home.

After she sends me to the office, I get someone to call Mom and tell her I'm sick and she needs to come get me. They are on the phone for a long time before the lady in the office hangs up and says I need to go to Jan's. I can't believe it. I thought for sure this would work. I cross the street and knock on the door and Jan sighs heavily and sends me to lay down in Clayton's room so I won't get any of the other kids sick. Mom must have called her and told her. I wish I hadn't done this. I hate Clayton's room. It smells awful and it makes me shiver.

I start a campaign to convince Mom that I'm grown up enough to not go to Jan's anymore. Katy and I need to stop going there. It's making us both sick. Besides, pretty soon it'll be summer, and Katy and I can't stay there all day. It will be too expensive. I already know how to start dinner and I promise Mom I'll make sure Katy has a healthy snack after school. I think it's the money that finally makes the decision for her. She says she has to give Jan a month's notice, but then we're free.

"C'mon!" I holler as I turn my head to look behind me. Katy is taking five-year-old steps through the alley, her backpack riding low and bumping along behind her. I am skipping home today because I have a plan. Mom has been so sad and tired lately and I know just how to cheer her up.

Even though Katy won't speed up, I'm not mad. I skip backwards and try to take her hand in mine, thinking that some of my excitement might make the leap from my fingers to hers. We have plenty of time. Mom will be at work until at least 5:30.

Tugging at the yellow yarn, I pull the house key out from under my sweatshirt. I am so eager to get inside that it takes me a few tries to get the key in the right way. Katy abandons her backpack on the porch and starts scratching at the thick grey paint on the concrete steps, picking it off in chunks. She flicks at a loose edge with her fingernail until she can slide one between the paint and the step and gently ease it off.

"You staying out here?" I ask.

She nods, her black hair shiny in the sunlight. I know how warm it would be if I put my hand there. I am so jealous of her silky hair. My hair is mousy brown and never does what I want it to. It's not totally straight like hers or totally curly like Chris's. It's just all wonky and weird and halfway in between. Just like me.

I bounce inside and drop my schoolbag on the floor in the hall. I'll deal with that later. Climbing up on to the counter in the kitchen, I pull down a book of recipes. As I crack the spine, I can already smell the gooey chocolate chip cookies. Mmmm, my mouth waters.

"Hee!" Mom is gonna get home from work and walk in exhausted to smell fresh-baked cookies. She is going to be so surprised!

I dig out a bowl and some measuring cups and begin. 2 cups flour. Scoop, plop, poof. 1 cup sugar. I love tilting the plastic measuring cup just a little to watch the tiny grains flow out and land on the pile of flour. Brown sugar, pack it in. Sticky fingers, but the sand castle shape in the middle of the bowl is so cool.

Eggs, butter, baking powder, salt. Hmmm, where's the salt? I hunt for the big blue cardboard container. Found it. Measure out the salt, pour it in. It flows in like the sugar. Cool. Chocolate chips. A few for the bowl, a few for me. A cup for the bowl, a few more for me. I stir and hum. Wait until Mom sees this! I hear Chris bang through the front door and drop his stuff.

"What'cha doin', short stuff?" He flings the refrigerator door open and stands there staring.

"Baking cookies for Mom. Wanna help?"

"Nope. I'm going to shoot baskets. Lemme know when they're done, though. I'll help eat 'em." He slams the refrigerator door shut and bops me on the head before heading out back.

"Hey, wait! Katy still on the porch?"

He is already gone. Crud, I better check on her and make sure she's coming inside. I put the spoon down and walk into the living room to see her twirling around in the gold chair.

"Hey, doll. Cookies will be ready in a little bit and you can have one when it's warm from the oven, okay?"

She nods and grins but doesn't stop turning.

I go back to stirring. Man, this is hard work. Will those yellow streaks of egg yolk ever blend in? Dang! I forgot to preheat the oven! Oh well, I have time.

I'd better check the dough to make sure it's all mixed right. It looks a little grainy. Ugh! Salty! Salty like the ocean! I have to stir more. I decide to use the electric mixer, even though it might destroy the chocolate chips, because I have to mix that salt in better.

I lift the beaters out of the bowl and run my fingers along them for one more taste. Salt. Oh, no! I had been so fixed on using the measuring cup for flour and sugar, that I put in a cup of salt instead of a teaspoon! Everything but my heart stops. I can't breathe. I screwed up big time.

I lift the phone receiver off the wall and look up the number we are only supposed to use for emergencies. I dial the bank and sit on the bar stool to stop shaking. I can feel my heartbeat in my throat and fingers.

"Mom," I blurt out as she comes on the line. "I'm so sorry. I really messed up. I decided to come home and bake you cookies as a surprise but I didn't pay enough attention to the recipe and I put in a cup of salt instead of a teaspoon. I wasted two entire eggs and a whole lot of flour and sugar and the chocolate chips are already mixed in and I used them all so I can't make any more cookies and I know we don't have very much money right now and I'm so sorry that I wasted all that food and I'll make it right if you tell me how to. I'm so sorry!"

"Um." I hear her take a deep breath. "It's okay, sweetie. It was a mistake. You are so sweet to do that for me. Just clean up the kitchen and we'll talk when I get home, okay?"

I am hot with shame.

"Okay, Mom. I'm so sorry." Tears are soaking my shirt collar and I can't see anything because it's all blurry and I'm so glad Chris went out to shoot baskets so he didn't see me screw this up. He would never let me forget it. The worst part is Katy, though. I promised her a cookie and now there won't be any. She has to know she can rely on me and right now I feel like I can't do anything right.

Tough

Daddy and Susan are getting married on May 30. It seems fast, but they have to, I guess, because Daddy is moving to Wyoming. He got a new job there and I feel like it's one more person leaving. He says that our family is growing because now we'll have Susan and her son, Tyler, but that's not true. They are moving two states away and that means I'll have less family, not more. Daddy says he and Mom talked a lot. He says they want all of us kids to come to Wyoming for the summer, that it will be easier for Mom to just work and not worry about us kids, and we can help him move into the new house and learn about the new town.

"We are all going to do some praying this summer. We won't be happy unless we do what God wants us to do," Daddy says.

I don't know what God has to do with this. I'm pretty sure God wanted Mom and Daddy to stay married, or the church wouldn't have kicked us out. I remember Mom saying it was God's plan for us to adopt Katy and Cameron, too, but I can't figure out why He would have let us love Cam and then take him away.

Katy is happy to go to Wyoming for the summer, but I'm not and I don't think Chris is, either. He doesn't want to leave his friends, and I don't feel good about leaving Mom alone with no kids. I feel like telling Daddy that I'm not going to go, that I'll stay here and take care of the house and the dog while Mom is at work, but that night I have a nightmare. In my dream, I'm standing on the porch watching a white van drive away with Cameron's face pressed up against the window, only it isn't Cameron, it's Katy and Chris and they're driving away from me and they won't look back and I know I'll never see them again. I can't let them go without me, but leaving Mom behind busts up the family, too. I don't know what to do and it's making me crazy. I don't pray about it, though, because I don't think that will help at all.

————

A few days before the wedding, Mom calls us kids out to the garage. You could eat off this garage floor if you wanted to. The walls are lined with hooks for sports equipment and yard tools. The pegboard where Daddy used to keep his tools is empty, but everything else is in perfect order. Daddy is here, but Susan isn't, which is weird. Ever since Daddy moved out, he and Mom are careful not to spend even one minute in the same place together without other adults. Now, they are sitting close to each other. Little moths nibble at my stomach, fluttering and biting until I want to slide out of the folding chair I am sitting in.

Daddy's half-ton wooden desk sits in the middle like an island and he is behind it on his old wooden swivel chair. I used to love to sit in that chair and turn slowly around and around until I got so dizzy I couldn't walk a straight line. Mom sits off to the side of the desk and Katy and Chris and I are in folding chairs facing them like naughty kids in the principal's office. I can feel the cold, thick vinyl against the backs of my knees and hear a peeling noise as I raise first one leg and then the other to unstick them.

Daddy clears his throat. His eyes are shimmery and his nose is a bit too pink. I have never seen him cry before and I don't want to see it today. Mom is sniffling and wiping her red-rimmed eyes.

"We want to talk to you kids," Daddy says, looking down at the desk. He rests his forearms on it and leans toward us. Talk to us? They don't talk to us. Chris and I have gotten good at huddling up from time to time to piece together information we gather, like crows with shiny treasures, but that's the only way we learn anything. They don't talk to us. Why now? The moths in my gut are pterodactyls.

"You know your father is moving to Wyoming." Mom is talking so softly I can barely hear her over the gnawing of the beasts in my stomach.

"And before I go, we have to decide custody, but we decided we don't want to put you kids through an ugly court battle, so we have agreed to joint custody." Daddy is using his official voice—the one we hear when he answers the phone or talks to people at work. Custody? What's that? I can't breathe.

"Joint custody means we have agreed to share you kids and you get to decide who you want to live with. We won't decide for you. Think about it and let us know," he explains.

Who you want to live with? Is this a test? How are we supposed to choose between our parents? Mom is so sad and fragile and she only ever wanted to be a mom. How can I leave her? But Daddy is the one I have been killing myself to please my entire life, and not choosing him might mean he will never love me the way I want him to. And what about Chris and Katy? If they choose somewhere I don't, I'm gonna lose them. I can't lose them, too. I have lost too much already. What am I going to do? We have until the middle of summer to decide, because wherever we go, they have to sign us up for school. The pterodactyls in my belly are having a feast.

————

Katy and I wear fancy yellow Jessica McClintock dresses and Susan lets us be in the wedding. I have a stomachache all day, imagining what Mom is doing home alone and how she feels about her husband marrying someone else. I keep trying to tell her I hate Susan and I won't go live with them, but she won't talk to me about it and lately, she won't really look at me. I don't blame her.

I do hate Susan. I figured out that if you hate someone, they can't hurt you when they leave. Also, if Daddy loves her instead of Mom, he can decide to love some other kids besides us and that is horrible. Maybe if he decides to love some other kids, then we should just stick with Mom. At least Mom knows what it feels like to be abandoned. It's probably not right to be thinking about this while Katy and I stand in the back of the church waiting for our cue to walk down toward Daddy, but I can't help it. I figure if I can help Mom at home and make things a little bit like they used to be, we can both feel less abandoned.

So far, I've learned to make chili in the Crock-Pot and Mom showed me how to make chicken and rice and tuna casserole so I can start dinner sometimes when I get home from school. Sometimes, Katy helps me make a salad, but mostly she doesn't and sometimes she freaks out for no reason and starts throwing things or poking herself with a pen or a stick. I don't know what is wrong with her, but she keeps talking about moving with Daddy and Susan. Chris says he hasn't decided yet, but I have to get them to both stay here with me. We are all going for the summer, but I hope we all come back again, even if sometimes Mom says she's so tired that we should just all go, that it's too hard and maybe Daddy can help with Katy more than she can. She says maybe Susan will stay home from work and be there all the time like Mom wishes she could.

"Your father ruined that for me," she says.

I stay quiet. I don't know if I'm supposed to say anything when she talks like this, but I decide it's not a question, so I won't get in trouble for not responding.

Finally, the music starts and it's time for Katy and me to walk down the aisle. The church is really pretty and it makes me a little sad that we don't go to church anymore. The wedding is over quick and Susan is excited to introduce us to all of her friends at the reception. I just keep trying not to think about what Mom is doing.

————

Daddy brings over boxes for us to pack things for Wyoming because there's a huge moving truck full of stuff going. He's grumpy about what we can take because he says his new house isn't as big as our yellow one.

"Pack all of your clothes and things. We will be there for the entire summer and you might decide to stay, so you might as well have as many things as you can. That way, your Mom won't have to send them later."

Yeah, right. I'm not staying. I don't even want to go. No friends. No Mom. For an awful minute, I fantasize that Mom breaks her leg or something and needs me to stay and take care of her.

When we're done packing, our bedroom seems really empty and I wander downstairs to find Mom. Susan says Mom went next door to see her friend Holly and I'm mad. I feel like Mom's ignoring us right now and I want to talk to her about my plan. I'm mad and that helps me get up the courage to talk about it, but I have to find her. Sometimes, I'm afraid to say things I know my parents don't want to hear because I don't know how it will go. Like, when I used to ask about Cameron or why Mom and Daddy got divorced, they got so upset with me. But I feel like I must be stupid because I can't always figure out what's happening, so I have to ask lots of questions to understand. When I do that, Daddy calls me a "chatterbox" and says "why can't you stop talking all the time?" Mom's arms get really heavy and hang low and her head dips down while she shakes it at me. They say it's too complicated or I'm too young and if I remind them how many times they said I was "mature" and "smart," they get mad.

But when I get mad, I get brave and my hands shake until I say what I have to say even if it means I get sent to my room or spanked. Sometimes it's enough to say what I think and hope they remember it later in case they want to. But Chris and Katy never ask questions and I think they must know that I'll do it for everyone or maybe they just don't get as mad as me. Maybe I'm crazy and I see things different than other people. Maybe all those times I thought something was a big deal, it really wasn't. Maybe all those times I thought someone was trying to hurt me, even though they said they didn't mean it, I was being "oversensitive." The more I watch people to try and understand where I am going wrong, the more I feel like I'm not *going* wrong, I just *am* wrong.

Maybe the truth really is different for everyone. Maybe it's normal to be one person at home and a different person at work or school. Maybe that is how everyone does it—just changing the story to fit the situation. Maybe me wanting things to be the same all the time isn't the way it really works.

By the time I get a chance to talk to Mom after Daddy and Susan leave with the big truck, she doesn't want to listen. She stands at the kitchen sink looking out the window to the backyard and she won't turn around to face me. She's scrubbing the egg off of the pan I used to make breakfast and slowly shaking her head back and forth. Her head is bent over the pan and I can just see past her to where Chris and Katy are playing H-O-R-S-E at the hoop over the garage. I'm glad they aren't here right now. If I can talk to Mom and she says my plan to get Katy and Chris to come back with me is good, then I can convince them.

"Go ahead and stay in Wyoming, Kari. It's okay. I'm going to be so busy here with work and the house. Call me anytime you want and send letters and pictures and come home for Christmas. Get a fresh start."

She doesn't have time for us anymore. She has a new boyfriend named Dallas and I think they're getting married, too. Maybe she wants a new family to love and a fresh start of her own. Maybe if you're abandoned, the best thing to do is just go find new people to love and start over. I'm not going to do that. I'm not ready to give up on Katy and Chris yet, and somebody has to show them that we are important.

———————

Driving to Wyoming is a lesson in shades of brown. I can't figure out why anyone would want to live here, especially after living in Oregon where it's green and there is water everywhere. It was really cool to see a giant herd of antelope racing down a slope when we drove around a corner, and Daddy is really excited to show us the Great Salt Lake, but when we get there, I'm not impressed. It is nice to get out of the car, though. Chris isn't talking to anyone and neither is Tyler. They both have their Walkmen on with headphones so Katy and I are trying to play games, but she gets carsick so most of the time her head is pressed against the window looking out. I'm trapped in the middle next to Ozzy Osbourne wailing and screeching because Chris's music is up so loud, and I have to pay attention so I can let Daddy know if he needs to pull over so Katy can barf.

By the time we get to the new house, I am really disappointed. The whole neighborhood is brand-new so there are only a few houses surrounded by empty lots and most of the houses, including Daddy's, sit like islands in a sea of dirt and dust and tumbleweeds. We are all tired of being in the car, cranky with each other from sharing space, and ready to explore, but there's nothing to see so we just start unpacking before it gets dark.

The next morning, I wake up to the *blap-blap-blap* of the roll shade sucking itself up, and bright, white light coming through the window. I can't remember where I am and when I look out the window while I'm lying down, all I see is sky. There are no trees, and it takes me a minute to remember that Katy and I are on the floor in our bedroom in the basement. Susan stands by the window in shorts and a tank top, smelling like cocoa butter. Her shoulders are brown and peppered with freckles and small spots where she has already sunburned and peeled this summer.

Katy doesn't move. She hates getting up in the morning and will fight you like the Tasmanian Devil if you try to force her.

We have a choice today: either we can help Susan in the yard or we can start unpacking boxes. But everyone has to get to work. We are a family now, she reminds me. I tell her I'll get Katy up and dressed and we'll meet her in the garage. If we help in the yard, at least maybe we'll get to see if there are any other kids in this neighborhood.

After a lot of bribing, I convince Katy to get up and I sneak into the kitchen to find a cookie for her to eat before we start working. We head out the sliding door to the backyard and Daddy shows us a picture Susan drew. Even though our yard is a brown rectangle, she has covered the page with curving edges and pictures of plants and Daddy wants us to make the yard look like that. I don't know how we will ever do that in this place. It looks like nothing grows here.

He says our first job is to find tumbleweeds and pitch them over the fence into the empty lot behind us, but half the time when we toss them, the wind blows them right back over the fence into our faces. This place is awful.

Daddy and Susan pound some wooden stakes into the dirt in a kind of hourglass shape in the front yard. It's hard work because this ground is so dry and hard and I watch as the curls at the base of Susan's neck get sweaty and start to drip. She works really hard and she's stubborn and I can't help but think how different she is from Mom and how weird this all is. Daddy and Mom never worked together in the yard. In our old life, there were boy jobs and girl jobs and I was the only one who sometimes got to do both.

Once they get all the stakes pounded in, they weave something called bender board through to make an outline for the lawn. Daddy says tomorrow the grass seed truck will come.

I sit on the step and munch on a sandwich and I'm surprised that I don't hate all of this. I miss Mom and worry about her a little, but I'm still mad at her for sending us away. I get up and go inside to get Susan a glass of ice water and when I bring it to her, she smiles at me even though I tell her that her back is starting to sunburn again.

Another way Susan is different from Mom is that she can't cook. She is worried about calories and healthy stuff so there's only Diet Coke in the fridge. Tonight, she is making something called chicken-fried steak for dinner and it sounds awful, but I know Daddy will make us eat it all. That hasn't changed.

After dinner, we call Mom and I feel funny telling her about what we did today. I don't want to hurt her feelings and remind her that she is all alone, but she seems okay. She says she and Dallas are getting married soon and they want to move to the beach for a fresh start. After she says that, I pass the phone to Katy because I feel like she just stabbed me in the stomach. I love our house in Klamath Falls and now, even if I go back to Mom, I won't be able to go back to my friends and my old bedroom. I'm losing everything. I wonder if that's why we had to pack everything in our rooms up before coming out here this summer. I wonder if Mom was just waiting for us to be gone to tell us she was moving. I go back and forth between wanting to cry and wanting to scream and throw something. I'm so mad and sad all at the same time that I can't even hug Katy when she gets off the phone and asks for a bedtime story. I tell her to ask Susan because I have to go take a bath and then I just sit in the bathroom for a long time.

After Katy and I brush our teeth, I ask Chris to come in to our bedroom for a minute. He stands in the doorway instead of coming all the way in because he doesn't want to talk to me. He knows I'm going to try and talk about Mom moving and he just wants to ignore it. Katy plays with a doll on the floor and I ask them if they're staying here or going back with Mom at the end of the summer.

Chris shrugs.

"Might as well stay here. Nothing to go back to, anyway. Dad said he'll teach me to drive soon, too."

I'm a little surprised because he has to share a room with Tyler if he stays here, but I kind of get it. It is hard to imagine what things would be like if we moved to the beach with Mom and her boyfriend. At least here, we get to help set things up. Katy agrees that she's staying, too, and so it's settled. There's no way I'm leaving the two of them.

Susan started a "swear jar" that we have to put money into every time we say a word she doesn't like, and at the end of the week she dumps all the money into the collection basket at church. It makes me crazy because that's our allowance in there, most of the time, and Daddy doesn't have to put money in there. If he did, the container would have to be a lot bigger because he swears all the time.

One Sunday we are totally bored at church and Chris grabs one of the short pencils they keep in the pews and a card for people to fill out and writes "THIS SUCKS!" on it. He passes it to me and I nod at him, but Susan sees. We're busted. She holds out her hand for the card but I shift my eyes away and pretend not to see her. She reaches across Katy and taps me on the shoulder and wags her finger at me. Her nostrils are big and her mouth is in a straight line that makes it look like she has no lips. Chris pokes me hard and shakes his head but I have to give it to her. I hand it over with the writing side down because he also drew Snoopy on the back, but we are doomed.

As soon as church is over and we get home, Susan calls Chris and me to the living room. I slowly change out of my dress and tights, hanging them up carefully in the closet, and I take a long time to choose a pair of shorts and a T-shirt. When I finally drag myself upstairs, I am shocked that Daddy isn't there with his hands on his hips. I crank my head to the side to look at Chris just as I hear the lawnmower start up and he shrugs at me and slumps down in the chair. Susan is sitting in the other chair across the glass coffee table and the card is sitting on the table in front of her.

"Your dad agreed to let me handle this. I just need to tell you how shocked I am that you two would act like that in church."

Now I'm more mad than scared. She is not our mom. What the heck is Daddy thinking, letting her lecture us like this?

"You need to be respectful, and this," she flaps the card at us both, "is NOT respectful. Were you planning on leaving it behind for someone else to find?"

Chris and I look at each other with huge eyes. We don't get it. We always doodle on those cards. The pencils are always perfectly sharp and Chris draws the best Snoopy and Woodstock I've ever seen. She never gets mad that we draw on the cards as long as we're quiet. So what if he wrote me a note this time instead of drawing a cartoon?

"People say 'this sucks' all the time, Susan. It's not a big deal." Chris can sound really sarcastic when he wants to. If it didn't piss people off so much, I might consider it his superpower.

"It IS a big deal, Christopher. Do you even know what that word means?"

Now, I'm really confused.

"That word—'sucks'—do you know what that word means? It refers to the act of a woman sucking on a man's penis. So, it IS a big deal!" Her face is turning red and her voice is really loud.

I look around to see if the windows are open because I don't want the neighbors or Daddy to hear. I want to throw up. What? What? Why is she saying this?

Chris coughs a little and I can't look at either one of them anymore. Daddy would NOT be happy if he knew Susan was telling us this. It would have been so much better if they had just grounded us or taken our allowance for a month or something. This is horrible. And I think Susan realizes it now, because she gets really quiet.

"Yeah. So that's why I don't like you saying that. That's why it's a word for the swear jar, and that's why you can never, EVER write something like that on a piece of paper at church. Ever." She rips the card into pieces, sweeps them off the glass-topped table into her hand, and stands up.

After she leaves, Chris and I sit there for a minute not talking or looking at each other until he snorts.

"What the hell? That woman is nuts!"

When he walks out to see if Daddy needs help with the lawn, I get the giggles and bury my face in the throw pillows on the couch to stay quiet. This life is crazy.

Katy starts third grade, I'm in sixth, and Chris goes to high school down the road with Tyler. I wish "fresh start" meant everything was easy, but Katy is still throwing tantrums a lot and it makes Daddy super angry. He spanks her all the time and Susan says she thinks they need a therapist to help. Daddy says she just needs to learn to act her age and we can't baby her anymore. I can't take care of her as much as I did at Mom's because Susan doesn't have a job and she's always around trying to be our mom.

Katy gets in trouble almost every single night for not finishing her dinner, and I don't really blame her. Susan cooks in the microwave a lot and the fridge has things like Miracle Whip and Velveeta cheese and Thousand Island dressing in it. Her food either has no taste at all or it tastes sour. Sometimes I wonder if Cameron would even eat this stuff, but I can't ask because he doesn't exist for anyone but me anymore. We don't have any pictures of him and Daddy won't talk about him and Susan never even met him. But I won't forget.

Katy is usually stuck sitting at the dinner table by herself after we are all done because she hasn't cleaned her plate. Daddy says it's her way of getting out of helping with the dishes after dinner, but I don't think so. After a few nights of sitting there for so long she falls asleep, she starts excusing herself in the middle of dinner to go to the bathroom and I'm proud of her until the time Daddy follows her and catches her dumping a napkin full of food into the toilet. If I try to speak up for her or help her somehow, I get yelled at, so I finally just start sneaking boxes of crackers into our bedroom closet so she can at least have something to eat when she's hungry.

Susan is trying really hard to figure us out and she convinces Daddy to send Katy to therapy, which I think is good, because she is either really sad or super angry all the time. I don't really know how to feel about Susan because it makes me feel like I'm betraying Mom if I like her, but despite her cooking, she is really funny and smart and she is very nice to me, even if she is a little weird. She has a great, loud laugh and she is really creative about the yard and friendly to everyone we meet. She is always asking questions about people's yards or kids and making new friends. Sometimes it's embarrassing that she's always talking to strangers, but she meets a lot of people that way and she has way more friends than the rest of us do since we moved here.

We get to call Mom once a week and I write her letters all the time and she says she's really busy trying to sell the house and move to Lincoln City with Dallas, who we will meet at Christmas. She says he is a writer and has a son who is a little older than Chris. Dallas has lung cancer, so she has to take care of him sometimes, but he's mostly healthy and she thinks we will love him. I feel pretty good that she has Dallas and she isn't alone, but she says she misses us a lot.

I want to tell her that Katy got caught shoplifting at the little store down the street from our house and Susan and Daddy are really mad, but I know it will just make her worry, so I don't. Even though Katy is going to a therapist, she still mostly only trusts me to calm her down when she's really upset and it makes me feel good to help her get up for school and make sure she takes a bath.

As soon as school is out for Christmas break, we pack our things for Oregon. I am excited to see Mom, but first we have to drive to Salt Lake City to get on the airplane. Daddy hands us off to a stewardess who says she will make sure we get to Portland. I'm a little nervous to fly without a grownup, but it's too expensive for us all to go and Daddy is going to stay and have Christmas with Susan and Tyler. He pulls me aside and tells me to keep an eye on Katy and make sure she doesn't get sick or cause problems on the plane and I promise I will.

Mom is crying when we get off the plane and walk toward her with our things. Katy is shuffling her feet because we flew overnight and it's hard to sleep on an airplane, so she is really tired. I hope she doesn't throw a fit.

"Hug Mom and I'll carry your stuff. You can sleep in the car cuz we still have to drive to the house."

She sticks her tongue out at me and runs to Mom.

Chris is already there, shaking hands with this huge, tall guy with a red beard. He has a big belly and twinkly blue eyes. It has to be Dallas, but he doesn't look like he's dying of cancer to me. He holds out his arms for a hug and I don't want to, but I hear Daddy's voice in my head telling me to Be Polite and Respect Your Elders, so I let him pull me in tightly and give me a kiss on the top of my head. It gives me the shivers.

His car is a big brown van with tools in the back. Mom explains that Dallas is a tool salesman and a poet and as soon as we are all piled in and she has her back to us, Mom says she sold the house, so we're going to Eugene to have Christmas at Dallas's house.

I hate not having Christmas in our own house. Dallas's house is a man's house. Everything is brown and cluttered and dusty and Mom says it's because he has cancer so he can't keep it up like he should. Also, it's just him and his teenage son, Kevin, who live there and cleaning up isn't a boy thing, I guess. Mom tells us that they're getting married in the spring and moving to the beach and I feel like she is getting a whole new life and leaving us behind. I mostly pay attention to Chris and Katy for the next few days and we play lots of card games. Dallas doesn't seem too sick, except he has coughing fits sometimes, so Mom doesn't really have to take care of him. I wish she would take care of us, but she's busy helping him pack things and get ready to move.

When we get back to the airport a few days later to fly home, I ask if we can come to the wedding but she says she thinks Daddy won't pay for it and she can't afford to fly all of us back and forth. I don't hug her very hard when the stewardess tells us it's time to go because I want her to know that I'm mad. I grab Katy's warm little hand and we follow Chris down the ramp to the plane.

We are almost the only ones on the plane because it's another red-eye flight. The stewardess feels bad for us so she gives us extra pillows and snacks. When she goes back to sit down and get some sleep, Chris bops me on the head with his pillow and Katy giggles. We start a huge pillow fight and then I open a package of peanuts and dump them on his head. The dust sticks in his curls and when he shakes his head, peanuts fly everywhere. Katy is laughing hysterically and I'm afraid that we are gonna get in trouble, but I'm tired of being the good kid. Sometimes, when the three of us are out somewhere by ourselves, which is a lot, I pretend that Chris and I are the mom and dad and Katy is our kid.

One of Daddy's favorite things to say is "Quit crying or I'll give you something to cry about." I don't get how adults even know what there is to cry about. Daddy yells bad words when he hurts himself and he isn't scared of anything. Mom cries all the time and Daddy says that's because she's weak. I want to show him that I'm tough, like the boys. Anyway, Wyoming is a place where you kind of have to be tough. Nobody wears pink or dances ballet. The girls all ride horses and wear Wrangler jeans and I want to show Daddy that I'm not weak like Mommy; I'm strong like him.

Now that they built more houses here, there are lots of kids on our street and we like to have water wars on hot days—there are a lot of hot days here in the summer. We hop on our bikes, arm ourselves with spray bottles and squirt guns, and chase each other up and down the steep hills, one hand steering and the other hand spraying.

A few older kids hide in the shadows with garden hoses and send geysers of water at us when we ride by. At first, being sprayed startles me, but the cool water feels really great and it's funny when kids jump out and holler. One boy named Jeremy who is in my class at school decides that he needs to attack me. He rides his bike straight at me and I'm so distracted by his tan, muscular arms and thick, sun-bleached curls that I forget to protect myself against whatever he's planning. He slams to a stop, handlebar-to-handlebar with me, and puts one hand out to block the spray from my bottle that I finally remembered to raise and aim at him. He hits the nozzle and the hard, plastic trigger digs into my hand and opens up a huge cut on my ring finger from the end of my nail all the way to the first knuckle.

"Hey!" I holler, hoping the blush I can feel spreading across my face can be explained away as heat-related.

He pulls his hands back and his clear blue eyes spread wide.

"Whoa! I'm sorry! Geez," he stammers and goes pale.

I shake my head, confused. He drops his bike and grabs both of my hands in his, stepping wide to avoid the blood dripping steadily from my finger.

"What?" I look down to see my hand soaked in red and my T-shirt sporting drops, too. "Oh, man. I guess I'd better go clean up. Move my bike out of the road for me?" I hadn't even felt it—didn't know I was bleeding. I walk down the hill toward home cradling my hand and I smile as I hear him telling everyone how tough I am—that I didn't even cry. I *am* tough. My finger doesn't even hurt. I guess you can get to a place where you can handle anything like it's no big deal. Maybe this is why some grown-ups don't cry.

Susan goes to the pantry to grab the first aid kit while I hold my hand over the kitchen sink, dripping blood on her favorite coffee cup. She is really gentle when she washes the cut and pours Bactine on it and that's when

I feel like crying, not because it hurts but because I'm trying to remember the last time Mom or Daddy did something like that for me, and I can't.

"Daddy, did you know Dallas is gonna die?"

I pestered Chris until he agreed to let me have shotgun since all he does is listen to his Walkman anyway, and I want to talk to Daddy on the way to the airport in Salt Lake.

"Hmmm, what makes you say that?" Daddy always drives with one hand slung over the top of the steering wheel and the other one on the stick shift. He's looking straight ahead at the road—probably to make sure no antelope come running out in front of us—and I'm looking at him. His thick hair shines almost red in the sun and his face is relaxed.

"Mom said he has lung cancer and he told her he is dying."

Dallas and Daddy are so different. Daddy is strong and fit and clean-shaven and always wears ironed clothes that smell like laundry soap. His shirt is always tucked in and his shoes are always shined. Dallas is scruffy, with a large belly and round cheeks and soft, frizzy reddish hair that hangs down past his ears. Dallas is clean, but he looks sloppy. Daddy would never go out of the house looking like that. Daddy is a businessman, and Dallas is a poet. Daddy has it all figured out. Dallas isn't even trying.

"He used to smoke, kiddo. That's what happens when you're a smoker. Sometimes you get cancer."

I feel better for a little while. Since Daddy and Mom don't smoke, that means neither of them will get cancer.

"Why did she marry him if he's gonna die soon?" I don't understand that part at all. She is always telling me that divorcing Daddy "ruined her life," so why would she choose someone new that she is just going to lose, too?

"We don't know if he will die soon, Kar. And she married him because she loves him." I guess that's what they call romantic—marrying someone even if you know they're deathly ill. I think it's stupid. If you can protect yourself from bad stuff, you should, especially from losing people. Hasn't Mom lost enough people?

Mom sent pictures of their wedding and Daddy said it looked "really hippie-dippie." He is right—there are flower crowns and they got married in a field by the beach. We are heading to Lincoln City for the summer and I decide to stay there to start junior high. Chris says he is going to stay, too, because he hated high school in Wyoming.

Katy says she won't come with us, but I'm going to spend the whole summer trying to convince her. I really want the three of us to be together.

Bootstrapping

The house in Lincoln City is pretty awesome. It's huge like our house in Klamath Falls was, with a big basement, and the kids' bedrooms are at the top like before, too. You can see the ocean right out the living room window, but Mom says don't get too attached because it's a rental. She had to split the money with Daddy when she sold the house in Klamath Falls and they didn't have enough money to buy a new house because Dallas quit his tool-selling job to move to the beach and write poems.

He has an office at the back of the house where he writes. He tells me that when he got cancer, he knew he wanted to spend the rest of his life writing at the beach, and I just nod my head. I like the beach a lot, too.

I keep waiting for Dallas to get really sick, but except for coughing fits every once in a while, he seems fine. He sits at his desk and writes poems and walks on the beach and cooks. He really is completely different from Daddy in every way except that he does that thing where he pretends he's teasing you and playing when he's really angry or being mean to you. Like when he forces me to eat a raw oyster even though I say I absolutely don't want to, and then he cackles when I gag and almost throw up.

Mom works all day showing houses to renters and people who want to move to the beach, and almost every night at the restaurant because you don't get paid to show houses, you only get paid when you sell them, and she doesn't sell very many. On Sundays, I go to the real estate office with her and help dust, vacuum, empty the trash, water the plants, and clean the bathrooms so she can make extra money. Sometimes when we're done, she sits down to study real estate stuff and I type letters to Daddy on the secretary's typewriter.

I hear Mom and Dallas fighting about money all the time because

Mom says Daddy doesn't ever pay his child support and Dallas isn't working except on his poems. He finally gets a job as a bartender and comes home smelling like cigarettes and alcohol and tells us stories about the guys who come in and drink beer and watch the whales out the back window. He hates his job and tells Mom that he would rather be writing poems. She says, "We need to eat," and points her eyes at me and Chris. Maybe things were easier for her when we were in Wyoming, but I can't go back now, so I try to help around the house as much as I can so she isn't so tired all the time. I wish I was old enough to get a job.

———————

I go out for the volleyball team, which means I have to start practice two weeks before school starts. It's nice because I get to know some other kids, but since I didn't play sports in Wyoming, I'm really sore after the first few practices. Sometimes, I groan when I have to walk upstairs to my room because my legs and butt are so sore. One night after the dishes are done, I ask if I can take a hot bath instead of going with Mom to show a house. Dallas tells her to go and says he'll take care of it and he tells me to lay down on the couch on my stomach. I'm still wearing my volleyball shorts and T-shirt and my kneepads are pushed down around my ankles. I lay down and feel the rough fabric of the old green couch up and down the front of my legs.

I figure he's going to bring me a hot water bottle or something but suddenly his beefy hands are massaging my legs and it tickles. I flinch and he tells me to relax. I don't want to hurt his feelings because he pouts for days if his feelings get hurt, so I start to sit up and say, "That's okay, I'll be fine. I'm too ticklish."

"I'm good at this. I won't tickle you. Lay down."

I'm not sure what to do. Chris is upstairs in his room with the music blasting and Dallas's son, Kevin, is in the basement smoking pot or something. I lay back down and turn my face to the back of the couch. He pushes his hands down the waistband of my shorts and starts kneading my butt cheeks and I can't breathe because I don't want this to be happening.

I hear the kitchen door open and Mom comes walking into the living room. "Geez, I forgot the slip of paper with the directions on it . . ." She trails off when she sees me on the couch.

Dallas struggles to stand up and pull his hands out of my shorts but he's so big that it takes him a long time.

I want to throw up. Or disappear.

"She was so sore. I thought I'd help her out with a massage." He leans over and slaps my butt and says, "There ya go, kiddo. That oughta do it. Get up."

I go upstairs without looking at either of them and ask if I can hang out in Chris's room for a while and listen to music with him. Now I'm really glad that Katy decided to go back to Wyoming. She is better off there.

––––––––––

It takes two years, but the year I start high school, Katy finally moves back to Oregon. Daddy and Susan have had enough of her troublemaking because I think she is still shoplifting even though they keep trying to get her to work with the therapist. I'm so excited she is coming back. Maybe Mom will be a little happier with all her kids here. Even though I've made lots of friends since we moved back, and Chris has, too, Mom still seems like she is always waiting for something horrible to happen. She has friends but she still works too hard at too many jobs, and maybe she still worries that Dallas could get sick and die anytime. Or maybe she just feels incomplete without Katy here.

Mom was right to tell me not to get attached to the beach house. It was too expensive, so we move to a smaller place with no view just up the street from Dairy Queen. I'm finally old enough to get a work permit, and I have a job at Dairy Queen with my friend, Angi. We make Blizzards and Dipped Cones and I smell like french fries when I get home until I shower the grease out of my hair. I slip money into Mom's wallet after I cash my paycheck because Dallas is back to not working again. He hated his job and tells everyone he's not doing well, so most of the time he either sleeps on the couch or takes off on some Mountain Man adventure somewhere, packing up his van with deerskins and piles of shiny antlers.

He and Katy either love each other or hate each other and I just try to stay out of the way. I'm pretty sure he is a total liar, that he never had lung cancer, and I'm tired of waiting for him to tell us the truth or die. I don't really need all the money I'm making because there's nothing to buy in this town except kites and saltwater taffy, and I want to help Mom. We never talk about it, so I wonder if she thinks the extra cash she finds in her purse is from tips she forgot she made at the Sea Hag.

––––––––––

Screams cut through the air. Barely muted by the closed bedroom door, they are shrieks of torment and rage. I struggle to get out of my waterbed, propping my calves against the wooden frame and pushing my hands down by my hips. My hands shove down until they hit the bottom. Shit—there's another leak somewhere. I tilt forward onto my feet and see Mom standing in my doorway looking tired and sad and defeated. My eyes meet her flat, hooded ones and she looks away. I say nothing and simply walk past her, smoothing her shoulder as I go to let her know I've got it.

The cheap doorknob turns easily and rattles a bit as I crack the door open. Even though it's a bright spring day outside, Katy's room is a cave. The shades are drawn, and the floor is strewn with clothes and magazines and stuffed animals. My eyes adjust to the darkness, and I take shallow breaths because it smells like fear and sweat and unwashed kid. I scan the shadowy piles of bedclothes and dirty laundry and finally find her in the corner of the room.

Katy sits slumped on a sour-smelling heap, toes protruding slightly from beneath her Strawberry Shortcake nightgown. Her hair is fixed in knots like blackberry brambles. She doesn't seem to notice that I'm there because there is no break in the deafening sounds coming from her lungs.

I pick my way through the mess to squat down in front of her.

"Shhhh, shhhh, baby. I'm here," I whisper. I know better than to touch her. She will recoil and let her anger fly like a cobra.

"Shhhh, shhhh, baby. I'm here," I repeat over and over again and as my voice begins to reach her, the screams become a throaty hum. I continue whispering and within minutes she is taking great hiccupping breaths. She won't look at me, but she shudders and shakes and tears drip steadily from her jaw, soaking the hem of her nightgown.

I sit down cross-legged on the pile of stuff near Katy and something sharp pokes me. I pull her onto my lap and settle her small frame in the hole I've created. She remains tightly curled and we rock back and forth as I murmur, "I'm here, sweetie. I'm here." I won't say the words "it's okay" because we both know it isn't.

After a while, her back uncurls like a fern, and I breathe slowly and deeply. I feel complete here like this, cradling her in my arms, soothing her. She lifts her chin to look at me and I smile softly as she slips her thumb into her mouth and a grin twitches as the corners of her lips.

"Hey," I say softly, "get that nasty thing out of there. You're too big for that, silly." She's almost as big as I am.

She smiles around her thumb as I wrap my fingers around her wrist and tug lightly. She lets a small giggle escape, and I increase the pressure. We play tug-of-war for a minute until she relents and a silver string of spit hangs like spider silk, a bridge from her full bottom lip to her wrinkly thumb.

"Whew! Got it!"

She giggles and slides it back in.

"Oh, no! Not again!"

We go through this routine once more and then she is ready to stand and brush off the crumbs of this morning's trauma. She feels safe for now, and I feel accomplished. I fixed it. Even if I don't know what "it" is.

———————

Daddy and Susan are moving back to Oregon and I'm glad they'll be closer. Now, maybe Daddy will pay child support to Mom because he doesn't have to buy plane tickets to visit us. Mom doesn't think that will happen, but it might. She is always worried about money, and I wish I could help more. Chris is applying to colleges right now, and I hear Mom and Daddy fighting on the phone about taxes and college and who will pay for all of it. Chris has been working at Lil' Sambo's for a few years and he is saving money, but Mom tells him that he has a college fund, so he shouldn't have to worry about it, but I think he still does.

I am eavesdropping one night when Susan calls to talk to Mom. I hear Mom ask if she can send Katy back to live there. It makes me sick to hear her talk about us kids like we're baseball cards that the adults can trade back and forth. Mom says she can't handle Katy and Susan says she understands, but she isn't sure there's anything she can do, either.

"Well, she trusted you enough to leave her diary lying around for you to read." Mom sounds jealous.

I don't know what that has to do with anything and I can't hear what Susan says in response, but I've had enough. I hope Katy never hears them talking like this and thinks nobody wants her. I want her. I love her. I just don't know how to help her.

———————

I hate that I'm ashamed of our house. Daddy and Susan's new house in Lebanon is really nice, but ours is a mess and it's only a rental. We live in a shabby little rambler with ugly shag green carpet full of crappy furniture like our 1970s orange-striped velour couch, with its variegated sunset colors. I hate that couch because it's a holdover from the divorce, another leftover that Mom ended up with. She got the house (and the mortgage), the new red Jeep Cherokee (and the car payments to go with it), the furniture, and eventually, Katy, when Daddy didn't want to handle her anymore. Daddy moved on to a new house, a new wife, and a new son. He got new furniture, a new town, a new car, a new life. We still have this ugly couch. Maybe Mom is right—maybe he did ruin her life. She is married to a guy who is a liar and a deadbeat, and we live here.

I turn the knob on the swollen, peeling front door and widen my eyes as I come into the dark living room. My eyes don't adjust as quickly as my ears do. For a second, with the door open, the sunlight glints off the sharp points of Mom's sewing shears as they slash through the air.

Katy comes up quickly behind Mom, screaming, "You aren't my real mother! I hate you! I want you to die!"

Mom is moving like she is underwater even though the scissors are mere inches from her back, and I want to scream at her. Nobody moves that slowly when they're in mortal danger. Katy, on the other hand, is a predator, quick and darting.

I dive between them, my backpack sliding off my shoulder with a thud that unleashes a cloud of dust. I manage to knock Katy off balance, and we sail through the air and land on the sunset-colored couch. The shears fly over the back and clang onto the linoleum in the dining room. Fear and hatred scrape and claw their way from my belly to my throat.

"Don't! You! Ever!"

I am straddling her on the couch, seeing only red. I have turned a corner, made an unthinkable pivot, and that is the only thing that stops me. I suddenly realize that I have my hands around Katy's throat and I'm shaking her. What am I doing? Until now, I have always protected her at all costs, but something broke in me today.

Quivering with adrenaline, I peel my hands from her neck and watch as fear turns to hatred in her eyes. The rage I feel fizzles and congeals into shame, hot and heavy in the pit of my belly. Dazed and dull, I slide off the couch and walk around to retrieve the shears, holding them by the sharp end like Mrs. Ludwig taught me. My hair falls away from my cheeks as I lift my head to see Mom frozen in place on the other side of the room.

I just saved her life, but she doesn't look relieved or pleased. She isn't acting grateful. She just walks past me like we are strangers in an airport terminal. As if we hadn't just flown in on the same damn plane with this suicidal pilot.

A week or so later when I ask her about that day, she feigns surprise. I want to know what set Katy off. Mom shakes her head and pats my hair and says maybe it was a dream. I recount the details with excruciating clarity, and she cocks her head and raises her eyebrows. The more she tries to deny it, the angrier I get until her nostrils flare and her mouth sets in a hard line.

"Enough, Kari. Stop talking about it."

I can smell her sweat and see the moisture collecting under her arms and the color rising beneath her orangey foundation. I don't know if it's because she does remember or if she won't. I don't know whether it haunts her that she knows what I know or if it frightens her to have convinced herself that events so vivid and terrifying didn't actually happen. In any case, she fails to take my side.

In that moment, it occurs to me that, more than anything, I want her to be my mother. I don't know why she feels like she needs to deny or squash or push my fears back on to me, but what I need most from her is solidarity. I need her to sit with me, hold my hand, and tell me that it's okay to be afraid. I need her to admit that this is not normal, that life is hard and crazy, and that I'm not the only one who sees that. I need her to show me that there is a beginning, middle, and end to all of this and that it is possible to wade through and come out wiser and stronger and farther down the path.

But she won't. And neither will Daddy. So, I keep circling back, grabbing first Mom and then Daddy by the hand, hoping to prove that what I see and feel is real, that it is there, and that I need help. But instead of believing me and offering to help, they say things like,

"That's not real."

"That's not my problem."

"What did you do to create that?"

"Ignore it and it will go away."

Neither of them says, "That looks terrifying! Here, let's go through it step by step together until we're on the other side."

Sometimes I fantasize about someone saying that—a teacher or someone else's mother or my boss, Kathy. But they'd have to know about my life first, and I can't tell them. I've spent so much time and energy doing what I was taught to do—pretend that everything is fine—that probably nobody would believe me if I told them what really goes on in my house. And then I wonder if I'd even know it if someone offered to help me because I'm so used to being on my own with all of this. I just hope I don't ever turn into the kind of person who makes other people feel like they're crazy when they are sad or scared.

When we go visit Daddy and Susan, Mom drives us to meet him halfway at a big mall parking lot in Salem. Daddy likes to park his car way out in the middle of nowhere so he doesn't get door-dinged and by the time we get there, we have to hustle to get back to his house in Lebanon in time for dinner, so we never get to go into the mall.

We meet Daddy on Friday night and Mom knows to park a few spaces away from him. Chris and Katy and I haul our stuff out of her car and dump it into Daddy's trunk, which is clean and empty except for his first aid kit. I almost forget to hug Mom goodbye and then I see how sad her face is. Dallas came with us this time, but he doesn't even get out of the car. He and Daddy don't like each other.

We have a pretty good weekend, eating ice cream and watching TV, and Susan is happy to see us again, but Tyler doesn't like us taking over the house he's had to himself. On Sunday morning, Daddy asks Chris to come help him in the yard, and I can hear them arguing out there for a long time. By the time we get into Daddy's car to go back and meet Mom that afternoon, Chris is refusing to talk to anyone. He shoves a tape into his Walkman and snaps it closed and glares at me. Katy and I climb in the back, and she rolls the window down so she won't get sick.

"I wish you guys could come earlier on Fridays. Lebanon High School has a great football team, and it would be fun to take you to a game." Daddy is trying to pretend that there's no tension in the car.

Chris snorts and mumbles that he's not ever coming back.

Daddy starts driving faster. Sitting behind Chris, I can see Daddy's nostrils flare and that he is strangling the stick shift. I'm really glad it only takes about half an hour to get to Salem. When we screech to a stop in the parking lot, Daddy yanks the hand brake so hard I think it's going to come off in his hand.

Chris barely waits for the car to stop before he throws off his seat belt and flings open the car door. Daddy leaps out to follow him and catches him at the trunk where he's grabbing his duffel bag. Daddy grabs Chris by the arm and turns him around so they are face to face. Katy turns to look out the back window, but I motion for her to sit back and stay in the car. I'm standing next to the door, keeping it open in case I need to duck back inside. Chris's face is redder than I've ever seen it.

"Don't TOUCH me, you hypocrite!" Chris screams and yanks his arm away. He whirls around and heads toward Mom's car a few spaces away.

"What the hell is wrong with you? You need to adjust your attitude, young man!" Daddy's hands are curled in to fists. He knows we're in public and he would never want to make a scene. He is shaking with the effort to control himself and sweat is forming on his brow.

Chris turns back to face him, heaves his bag up onto his shoulder, raises both middle fingers in an angry salute, and screams as loud as he can, "FUCK YOU! JUST FUCK YOU!! I'm never coming back here!" And then he's gone, disappearing inside Mom's old Buick, staring straight forward and not moving. The air shimmers with heat and rage.

By the time Daddy turns back around, Katy has climbed out of the car. Even though his forehead is covered in sweat and he is still shaking, Daddy flashes a big smile at Katy and me and opens his arms wide for a good-bye hug. He folds us both in and kisses us on top of our heads before grabbing our stuff from the trunk and handing it to us. My face is hot, and I'm trembling. I've never seen Chris show that much emotion.

I don't know what happened, but I'm sure it has something to do with money and college. Mom is always telling us how Daddy never pays her for child support, and he claims us on his taxes, and he ruined her life. She says that he made her all sorts of promises that he never kept, and he's gonna do that to us, too, so we'd better watch out.

But she's the one who sent us away to Wyoming, and she won't tell me what happened to Cameron, and she's the one who married Dallas and lets me take care of Katy all the time, so I'm not sure Daddy is one hundred percent at fault. Before, my anger helped me have the courage to ask questions and speak up, but somewhere along the line I gave up and now I'm mostly just worried all the time. I know it's not worth it to try to force my parents to give me answers anymore, so I'm just using my anger to help me count the days until I'm out of here.

My Turn

'm finishing my junior year of high school, and Chris has been away at college for two years. Not much has changed except that I can drive now, and I work at a big fancy resort and make more money than I did at Dairy Queen.

The problem with taking care of Katy is that the more I do it, the more I have to do it. Even though she is in junior high now, it sometimes seems like she's stuck back at eight years old. Sometimes she gets so angry it scares me, and other times she just cries and cries and I don't know what to do. I'm so tired.

She has started running away, which really freaks me out, both because I don't want to lose her and because I'm afraid it will convince Mom to send her to live with Daddy. The first time it happens, I call my friend Mike to come help me look for her because if we can find her before Mom has to ask for help from the cops, maybe it won't be a big deal. Over the next few months, I assemble a rotating cast of friends to help me track her down when she goes missing. I have a phone tree of sorts that is both secret and wide-ranging, and we always manage find her. To me, this means that she wants to be found, and every time I look for her, I'm proving how much I love her.

Katy fights Mom every time they go to therapy, so they finally stop going at all. I wish I could help, but she won't really talk to me about any of the stuff that's really bothering her. She gives me glimpses every once in a while—dark, depressing poetry she writes, scabs on her arms where she cuts herself sometimes, letting me give her a ride home from a high school party she went to—as long as I don't preach or try to change her. All I can do is love her. I'm not going to fix this, but I can't shake the sense that somehow, I'm doing it all wrong.

One day when I don't have to work after school, I let myself into the house and realize it's empty. Chris is off at college, Katy is God-knows-where, and Dallas has moved to a little town in Eastern Oregon where he can live out his Mountain Man fantasies full-time. Mom is showing property, and it's really quiet and creepy to be in the house all alone. I walk through the kitchen and realize that the impression I have of Mom is that that she's always gone. It's like a footprint showing evidence that someone was once there, but they're not now. The Crock-Pot filling the house with the smell of spaghetti sauce, or a clean load of laundry piled on the couch to be folded is proof of her existence, but if she is home, she's locked away in her room with the shades drawn and the lights off. More often than not, she lies down for a nap before dinner and gets up to sit with us for a few bites before disappearing again.

I suppose I should appreciate the freedom it gives me. I ought to be thrilled that she is so easily swayed toward my point of view on how late my curfew should be or if it is wise to work 40 hours a week and play volleyball while going to school full-time, even if it is because she's too tired to argue, but on the nights when Katy flies into a rage or runs away or I'm just feeling lonely and depressed, I wish for a mother.

There are nights when I bury my face between two pillows so that my rough, racking sobs won't bother anyone, and all the while, I'm secretly hoping she will hear me from across the hall and come running.

During the day, nobody would ever know. I'm an almost straight-A student, and I'm a peer mentor and on student council. My boss at work knows she can count on me to do whatever she needs—be the hostess one night and bus tables the next. I even run room service orders when things are busy and someone doesn't show up for work. I play sports and tutor a blind student in biology and sing in the choir, and my life is under control when I'm not with my family. Except for the fact that I never eat lunch. Ever. Sometimes, I leave campus with my boyfriend or a group of his friends and they always stop at McDonald's or Quick-Mart to get chicken and jojos, but I won't let him buy me lunch and I feel funny about him watching me eat, so I always say I'm not hungry. Mostly, by the time I get to work, I can't wait to duck into the kitchen and eat a huge bowl of clam chowder with sourdough bread before I pass out from starvation.

In lots of ways, my life seems perfect. My boyfriend is the quarterback of the football team. All my teachers love me, and I have lots of friends. But even my boyfriend doesn't know how different my other life is. I have to work hard to stay in control by not eating in front of him and matching him grade for grade and paper for paper so that he will never suspect I'm not good enough for him. His parents are pillars of the community, and his brother is in the Naval Academy. If anyone really understood where I come from, they would know I don't belong with him.

But then, halfway through our junior year, he breaks up with me for no apparent reason. We never fight. I always defer to him when it comes to which movie to see and where we should go on Friday nights. The only thing I won't do is have sex with him—at least not all the way. I'll do lots of other things, but I'm not doing that. It's all part of being in control. I don't drink or smoke pot, either, and I don't want to. We like the same kind of music, and I watch every football and basketball game, except when I'm at work, so what is it? He won't tell me. All he says is that he thinks we need to take a break, and I don't know what that means. Unfortunately, we have almost every single class together, and our lockers are in the same hall, and we have all the same friends. Our high school has less than 400 kids in it, so it's impossible to not see him every day, but the notes I slip in through the vents in his locker go unanswered, and he won't make eye contact with me.

After weeks of crying and questioning his friends who just shrug their shoulders, I decide it was because I wouldn't sleep with him. Rumor has it, he's already started to see the new French exchange student, and then one night, my friend Mike says he saw him at some party giving Katy some drugs, and I'm done with him. I don't even mourn the loss anymore. He can have his life filled with girls who will have sex with him and pretend that he and I haven't been best friends for over two years. I was sad and shocked, but the news that he is helping Katy destroy herself just makes me realize I guess I never knew the real him, either.

My next boyfriend never stood a chance. By the time we started dating, I was determined that this relationship would be a fling—something fun and completely different. After my last relationship blew up, I figure the key this time will be to have fun and be in control of not only myself, but all the rules of engagement, too. I am a teacher's pet, student council rep, college-bound responsible type. Jesse doesn't care much for school except as a social endeavor or a place to smoke pot, and he doesn't pay much attention to details. At first glance, he's a tough-guy skater, and I am a girly girl, but first glance is wrong. I know tough. Tough isn't something you do in front of everyone else. Tough is what happens behind closed doors that you take care of and don't talk about.

We are both seniors in high school, and we work together at the same five-star resort. We flirt in an easy, noncommittal way and everyone is shocked when we start dating. Jesse is cute in a skateboarder-rebel kind of way and, to be honest, I love that we are creating a stir. I'm off to college soon, and I can finally see my way through to freedom, so this is a bit of fun after all my years of hard work. A giant fuck-you to the world of responsibility and rules, at least until I graduate and move away and never look back.

I lose my virginity in the front seat of his Subaru Justy parked in the dark driveway of his mom's house. There is no risk of getting caught since she lives in a gated community and the driveway is at the bottom of a long, dark flight of stairs from the house. I fight with the stick shift for space—a maneuver that will result in a bruise on my left hip that lasts a week. We didn't plan it so we don't have any protection. I don't remember how long it lasts or whether I enjoy any of it, but I am relieved that it is done. Virginity gone—check.

Because I'm not willing to think about this relationship lasting very long, it never occurs to me to go on birth control. And even if it had, I would never have been able to get anything besides condoms without my mother's permission, and that isn't going to happen. I prefer to live day by day, staying unattached and having a good time, which works for a while, until Jesse's stepfather shoots himself in the head during an argument with Jesse's mom.

After that, Jesse moves into Chris's old room because, at first, his mom is in a treatment facility. Then she decides she can't live in Lincoln City anymore. That's when the fun stops. All of a sudden, Jesse becomes one more person for me to take care of, and I can't break up with him because his whole life has just exploded. I am horrified at what happened, and I feel so awful for his mom, but I also feel trapped. I finally got to the point where I could imagine my life on my own, and this wasn't part of the plan—to have a boyfriend who literally lived in my house. I tell myself it won't last much longer. Graduation is in six months and then he will move to California to be with his mom and I am off to college.

———————

I am accepted to three colleges in the spring, and my countdown calendar makes me happy every single day. I can't wait to get the hell out. Katy has all but dropped out of school, and Jesse moved in with a friend from work because I won't let him smoke pot in Chris's room. I keep thinking about breaking up with him, but I'm too much of a coward so I decide to wait until graduation. The timing will be so much better because we'll both be moving. Nobody stays together when they go off to college. And, for now, I have some breathing room, even though we still see each other at school and work and when his car breaks down, which is often, I drive him to school and work. He swears he loves me, and it makes me really uncomfortable, but I convince myself it's just that he's appreciative because when he needed me, I was there. Like Stockholm syndrome. Once he moves back to California with his mom, he'll forget all about me.

One morning when I stop by his new place to pick him up, I am halfway up the porch steps when I'm overcome with nausea. My mouth fills with hot saliva and I lean over the railing to puke in the bushes.

Shit. Am I pregnant?

At lunchtime, I beg off joining my friends and drive to the drugstore for a pregnancy test. Slipping into a stall at Dairy Queen, I unwrap it as quietly as possible. Tons of girls from school are touching up their lipstick in the mirror. This town is too small for me to risk anyone hearing me open this thing. I pee and sit to wait, wishing they would all just go. I hear the door creak open and their voices fade just as the pink plus sign materializes in the window of the stick. Dammit. Three weeks until graduation and I'm pregnant. What the hell am I going to do?

"We could get married, if you want." Jesse sits on the end of my waterbed that night, wringing his hands and flipping his hair out of his wide, fear-filled eyes. "You could still go to college while I work. I bet our baby would be one cute kid."

I suppress a harsh laugh. I have totally checked out of this relationship. My head is two months in the future when I'll pack up and head to college and never look back. I am furious with myself for being in this situation. It's just one more example of how messed up things get when I do things I don't want to do for other people.

"That's crazy. We are too young, and this is not what we want our lives to be. I'm having an abortion."

————

Making the appointment is simple. All I have to do is pull out the yellow pages and look under "Abortion Services" to find a clinic in Portland. There are no Saturday appointments available for the next few weeks, so if I want this to be over before I deliver a graduation speech to my peers and collect my diploma, I'll have to skip school. I choose to miss out on Senior Skip Day and make an appointment for eleven o'clock in the morning.

Coming up with the cash isn't hard, either, because I make good money in tips at work. I tell Jesse it's going to cost $250, and he whines about rent and buying his own food and gas, so I tell him to just give me $50 and we'll call it even.

On the day of the appointment, I get up and shower, put on my newest pair of underwear and head out like I am going to school. I park at Jesse's, puke in the bushes, wipe my mouth with the back of my hand, and knock on the door. I don't really want company for this, but the receptionist said I should have someone drive me, and there is no way I am telling anyone else but him.

He opens the door of his Justy and pecks me on the cheek as I slide in. It is pouring rain for the first part of the drive, and I keep my eyes peeled for deer. The road is lush and tree-lined, and I know more than one person who has hit a deer along this winding twelve-mile stretch known as the Van Duzer Corridor. Because of the weather, I don't feel very bad about missing Senior Skip Day. I wonder what the other seniors are gonna do if it rains all day.

About five miles in to the corridor, Jesse's piece-of-crap car begins to splutter and jump, and we look at each other and swear. He pulls into the parking lot of Marshall's, the only restaurant for miles. They're known for their cinnamon rolls that are the size of dinner plates and boast enough frosting to choke an elephant, but right now, we are the only ones in the parking lot. Jesse maneuvers the car around the enormous puddles in the gravel lot as my mind races to come up with options. Most of our friends are at Senior Skip Day so we can't call them. We finally agree to call Jesse's roommate Pete, but he says it will be at least an hour before he can get here. There's no way I'm making it to the appointment in time today.

When I get home, I make an appointment for the following Tuesday and insist that we take my car this time, as much as I hate letting Jesse drive it. We make the trip in less than two hours, park in a city lot across the street from the clinic, and poke our folded dollar bills into the slot to cover what we hope is enough time. We make our way through the knot of protestors holding signs with gory photos and handing out flyers. We're an easy target—a teenage girl with her deer-in-the-headlights boyfriend. Jesse can't help himself and gets defensive with one of the pro-lifers, snatching a flyer and tearing it up in his face, but I walk steadily forward and push open the glass door. He is going to have to catch up.

The waiting room holds a few girls my age, a few older women in their 20s and 30s, and one petrified young teen, white and shaking, sitting with her thin, unshaven father. He rests his arm around her protectively, and his cheeks hang low in sadness. His eyes are soft and loving as he watches me walk in the door and check in. I want to go sit with him and ditch Jesse. Jesse is useless. His eyes are huge and frightened, his palms are sweaty, and he is breathing in quick, shallow pants that make his nostrils flare.

I slide the cash into the trough beneath the thick Plexiglas and fill out my paperwork standing at the counter. When I finally sit down, I tuck my hands between my knees and rock back and forth to soothe myself.

When the nurse calls my name at the door, I stand up and walk toward her without looking back. I can't worry about Jesse anymore.

After I pee into the plastic cup and hand it to the nurse to verify my pregnancy, she directs me to a room and says to undress and put a gown on. The room is freezing and I wonder whether "undress" means I can leave my bra on or not. I finally decide they are only interested in the lower half of me, so I remove my jeans and fold them, tucking my best, cleanest underwear inside to conceal them on the chair. I lay my T-shirt on top gently and put the gown on with the opening in the back and sit on the stiff, crinkly paper that covers the exam table. I've only ever done this once before for a pap smear, and it was humiliating as hell.

The nurse finally comes back in and asks me to lie down and fit my heels into the stirrups. My legs are made of dried Play-Doh that stiffens more and more by the minute. My knees are shaking so I tip them together in an effort to steady them.

The doctor swings open the door and sits down on a stool between my legs. I can barely see the top of his head over the tented gown. The nurse stands next to a tray of tools on wheels and I look away, up at the ceiling, grateful for tiles to count.

The doctor's calm voice interrupts my count. "I need you to relax."

I can't reply. I left my voice out in the waiting room. The nurse leans over and puts her warm, soft hand on my shoulder, which makes me shiver.

"Your bottom needs to be touching the paper. That will help you open your knees a bit more."

I hadn't even realized my butt was hovering in the air.

I try to relax. I picture it in my mind. I force my knees apart. I will it to happen, but my butt still won't touch the paper. My body is refusing to cooperate.

"I can't do this if you don't relax." He sighs. His voice sounds soft and kind, but I know he's annoyed with me.

The trouble is, I don't know what "this" is. I have no idea what to expect. Cold? Sharp pain? What will it sound like? Will I feel the bleeding? Will it run out of me and be sucked up or will it fill up the trench between my legs like a warm river, puddling onto the paper and running off the table? My tongue is stuck to the roof of my mouth and I can't move any part of my body save my eyes. I am using all of my energy to keep myself in my head, to hold back tears, to not scream.

I don't know how long they wait, but at some point, the doctor slides his stool back and stands up. I look into his blue eyes as he cocks his head.

"I'm sorry. There are lots of other girls waiting outside, and we can't wait any longer. I can't do this if you can't relax."

A thick mass blossoms in my throat and my lips remain glued together. My eyes fill with tears that run out the sides and across my cheeks and fill up my ears. I can't do anything but nod. He turns and walks out of the room.

I feel the nurse's hand on my shoulder again and turn to look at her.

"We have an anesthesiologist who comes in twice a month. Why don't you make an appointment to come back then and you can just be asleep for the whole thing? He'll be here next Wednesday."

I don't remember getting dressed, but somehow I'm back out in the waiting area. I have to make another appointment but I hate having to talk loud enough to be heard through the thick barrier. I am mortified. What the hell is wrong with me? Where is my tough-girl attitude now?

I can't bear to admit how pathetic I am, so I lie and tell Jesse that the doctor said my uterus was tipped backwards, which means they have to do it under anesthesia. The receptionist explains that if I am going to do it that way, I need to plan to spend the entire day at the clinic to allow for recovery time. Good. That means Jesse can just go hang out in the city, and I won't have to be in the back picturing his sad puppy-dog face in the waiting room.

I have to come up with an extra $300. Time to pick up some extra shifts at work and come up with another excuse to miss school.

The following Wednesday I find myself back in the same exam room, but this time my stomach is completely empty and my nerves are more settled. *Third time's a charm*, I think wryly. But maybe I shouldn't have thought that, because that's how many tries it takes to get the IV in me. In the end, they can't find a vein in my arm or my hand, so the line is sticking out of the top of my foot. At least, once they get it going, I am asleep almost instantly and wake up later in a quiet room lined with rows of beds where a few other women lie in different stages of waking up. My mouth is dry and fuzzy and the lights on the ceiling seem to sway back and forth, but I am thrilled to notice that I feel mostly fine. A nurse brings me some ice chips to suck on and cautions me to go slowly.

"We put your underwear on with a big pad. You'll bleed for a few days—mostly spotting. If you get a fever or severe cramps, we want to know right away. But you were pretty early, so you should be just fine. We wrote everything down for you."

I have no sense of time and there are gaps in my memory, but at some point, I'm sitting somewhat gingerly in the passenger seat of my own car, my head pressed against the cool window. Jesse keeps glancing at me until I bark at him to stop and pay attention to the road. It's raining and we are in the city. I just want to get home without any more mishaps.

We agree that he will take me to his place because I can't risk Mom seeing me all doped up like this. She would assume I was on drugs and lose her mind. I have to sleep it off at his place until I am ready to go home. I thought ahead and told her I had to work until 10, so we have plenty of time.

Once I've had a cup of chicken noodle soup and a long nap, I am ready to go. I test my feet to make sure I'm not still woozy and grab my keys.

"Are you sure you're okay?" Jesse has been hovering over me all afternoon, making me crazy. I can tell he wants details, but since he didn't cough up any more money and I only had him along because I was forced to, I'm not telling him a damn thing.

"I'm great. Honestly." I'm a little surprised to realize that I mean it. I have just become my own knight in shining armor. I fucked up and I fixed it. I took care of myself for once—put myself first. I know it sounds weird, but I'm proud of myself. Next up, college.

After my abortion, the weeks fly past. I finish up school, deliver a speech along with the other valedictorians and salutatorians, accept my diploma and Honor Society certificate, and spend the summer working and saving money. Susan and Daddy got a divorce after a long, ugly dispute so I don't even go to Lebanon to visit them. Susan caught Daddy cheating on her and she and Mom bonded over stories of the horrible things Daddy did to each of them throughout the years. They have become friends of sorts and call themselves "The Survivors of Dick Club," which they think is hilarious because Daddy's name is Richard.

I am not sure what to think of this, because Mom seems to want to tell me awful tales about Daddy. It's as though Susan has rekindled this fire of hatred inside her and she suddenly has more energy, but it's hard to know what to believe. Some of the things she says don't seem right, I can't imagine my father doing or saying some of the things she claims he did, and since she always did have a different idea of what was Real than I did, and Daddy isn't here to defend himself, I mostly feel sick. I tuck the details away in my head in case they complete some puzzle I am curious enough to put together in the future and decide that, right now, the most important thing is for me to get out and start my own life.

———

When I leave for college, I steel myself. I will not be responsible for anyone else ever again. I am not getting married. I am not having children. My heart is still tender, but it lies beneath a rigid shield. I am packing the last of my things and trying to decide whether to take my Thompson Twins poster or not as Mom comes to stand in my doorway.

"I'm gonna miss you, you know," she says softly. I look up and take in the fact that we're the same height now. When did that happen? Her reddish, color-treated hair is thin and her mouth droops down at the corners in a near-permanent frown. She leans against the door frame in exhaustion.

"You're gonna have to figure out what to do about Kate." It's all the response I can muster. "It won't be easy. She will hate it there, with Dallas." Mom has decided to give him another chance, hoping that if she moves, Katy can go back to school in a town where nobody knows her and maybe that will make things easier. Yet another "fresh start." Mom says she wants to see if she and Dallas can make a go of it. He found some cabin in the woods that he has decorated with antlers and animal skins and a woodstove, and I can't picture her living there like that, but she doesn't want to be alone and I guess I don't blame her. I wonder if she's admitted to herself that he was always full of shit with that lung cancer stuff, that he was never dying, and then I realize I don't care. I'm out of here.

———

I end up at the same university where Chris is a senior, and we see each other on campus every once in a while. It reminds me of the days at Roosevelt Elementary when I saw him across the playground and felt whole. We don't even go see Mom for Christmas my freshman year. We don't go to Daddy's, either, because he has a new girlfriend that we don't really know and I'm still not sure how I feel about him. I talk to him every once in a while, and see him when he comes up to help me buy my books, but it's hard to erase the questions in my mind, especially when I figure out that the new girlfriend is the one he was cheating on Susan with. Ironically, Susan lives in Salem now, which is only about 25 minutes from where Chris and I are, so because there's a ton of snow on the pass between us and Mom, and Daddy is spending the holidays with his girlfriend and her three young daughters, we head to Susan's. Chris and Tyler and Susan and I are reunited in a weird jumble of chosen family and it's the easiest Christmas I can ever remember, despite the fact that occasionally I have to push the idea of Daddy going and finding himself another new family out of my head.

Mom calls us at Susan's on Christmas morning and I tell her I love her and talk to Katy for a while. I was right: she hates it there. The town is even smaller than Lincoln City and she hates living in that smelly, smoky cabin. I am torn between feeling like a horrible person for leaving her and reveling in the freedom I have to just focus on my own life right now. I miss her terribly and I wish that she was happy, but I'm beginning to understand that no matter how hard I worked for all those years, I wasn't making her happy, either. I didn't have the power to change our lives enough to make a difference. I only had the strength to keep putting out fires, and while that was better than nothing, I still don't have any magical way to fix anything. I have to find a way to move forward.

My life is full of classes and work. I have a work-study job as a math tutor and I'm also working in a veterinary clinic. I'm on a pre-med track and want all of the practical experience I can get, so I wake up at four o'clock in the morning and let myself in to clean cages, feed animals, and administer medications. On weekends, I assist with spay/neuter and tooth extraction surgeries, but I especially love the emergency cases. The combination of blood and adrenaline somehow calms me and sharpens my mind. I can hold a terrified kitten and whisper soft, calming words in its ear while the vet draws blood or inserts an IV. I stand on a stool and steady a horse's head and gaze into his eyes without flinching as a huge rasp files down the molars that have gotten too sharp.

Things are going great except that Jesse followed me to Portland instead of moving to California with his mom. He lives 15 minutes away with a bunch of his stoner friends, and they all work at the same restaurant, washing dishes. They skateboard and snowboard and smoke pot, and he calls me all the time. I was too chicken to break up with him for real, so now I mostly avoid him or tell him I'm working or studying. I'm going to have to break it off soon, but every time I talk about it, he threatens to kill himself and that's the one thing I can't be responsible for, so it's easier to just stay together for now.

I also have a roommate who is pretty awful, but I don't really feel the urge to take care of her. She is always losing her things in a musty pile of laundry she never washes and she can't write a coherent sentence to save her life. She sleeps until noon and fills the rest of her day with equal parts soccer and alcohol, but she's not my problem. I keep my side of the room tidy and organized and do my best to overlook her penchant for swiping my cottage cheese from the minifridge because I don't want to have to solve any problems beyond the ones my professors dole out.

Mom falls and breaks her collarbone in the spring, so Chris and I head over the mountain pass to visit her in the hospital. I wonder, all the way there, if she fell or if Dallas hurt her. When we stand next to her bed, she looks embarrassed and I can't bring myself to ask her. Anyway, what would I do if he had hurt her? It's up to her to leave if she wants to. I realize how good I'm getting at building a wall against the concerns I have for her and Katy. We spend the night in Dallas's smoky, dark Mountain Man cabin and over breakfast, Chris and I quietly agree that now that we know Mom is okay, it's time to go.

One day, my friend Sean offers to let me use his Bi-Mart card if I want to. I need shampoo, but it's so expensive at the grocery store, and he says if I take him with me, he'll let me use his card to get in. He's a year older than me, but I've been tutoring him in calculus, and I think he has a crush on me. He's cute in a traditional Irish-boy way with his stocky frame and blue eyes and big smile, but I still haven't broken up with Jesse, even though I've been trying to. We head out to the little parking lot near my dorm and I walk to where my car should be, but it isn't there. Sean starts making fun of me, saying that maybe he shouldn't trust me to help him with math if I can't even find my own car in the parking lot, and I'm about to shoot him my best disgusted look when I see it. Jesse's crappy little car is parked right next to where I left my car last night. Jesse stole my car.

I don't have a phone in my dorm room, but Sean does, so he offers to let me use it when he realizes I'm not kidding about my car being stolen by my boyfriend. My soon-to-be ex-boyfriend, I tell him. We walk across campus to his dorm and when Jesse answers, I try not to embarrass myself in front of Sean.

"You have to bring my car back. Why did you take my car? What the hell is wrong with you?"

"I'll bring it back if you talk to me. Face to face. You've been avoiding me and I'm tired of it. I'll bring your car back if you agree to meet me in person to talk."

"No. You stole my car and I'll call the cops if you don't bring it back. You don't get to blackmail me into talking to you. That's crazy and this is part of why I'm avoiding you. Bring my car back now or I'm calling the cops."

If I weren't standing here with Sean right now, there's no way I'd have the courage to talk to him like this and it makes me sick to my stomach to admit that. I would totally cave to Jesse, agree to coffee or something, if I weren't trying to seem tough for Sean, but the fact is, I set out to reinvent myself and erase my past when I came to college and if this is what I have to do to be a stronger, more independent person, than I will. My ace in the hole is that Jesse is terrified of the cops. He knows if I call them, he's screwed. Most of his stoner friends have been busted for drugs or petty theft at least once, and I doubt his car tabs are up to date. What I didn't count on is what comes next. He starts crying.

"If you break up with me, I'll kill myself. I swear I will. You're the best thing in my life. You're smart and pretty and I love you. You make my life better. I need you. Just meet me and talk to me. Please. I'll drive over now. I'll bring your car back, but you can't break up with me."

"Bring it back." It's all I can say before I hang up and start shaking. Sean's eyes are huge. He moves closer to put his arm around my shoulder and asks what I'm going to do.

"I don't know. He said he'll kill himself. And I think he will."

Sean doesn't know anything about Jesse's stepdad or his mom, and he doesn't know about all the shit I went through with Katy. That's not part of who I am here, so nobody knows. I am worried that Jesse might do something stupid, but I can't stay with him anymore. It will destroy me. I came here to get away from taking care of him and Katy and Mom. I don't want that life anymore.

"No, he won't. He's just saying that. And if he did, that would be his choice, not your fault. You can't control what he does. Do you want me to come with you to the parking lot?" His arm is still around me, and I realize it's the first time in a long time I've felt protected by someone else. Even though I know he has no idea what Jesse is capable of, I decide not to challenge his interpretation.

I nod because I know if I open my mouth again, I'll start crying. I can't believe how calm and cool Sean is through all of this. He's a year older than me and I know he calls his parents every single Sunday. His sister works on campus and they're really close. That's the kind of family I wish I had. Instead, my life is still so messed up. Who gets their car stolen by a crazy boyfriend on this tree-lined private school campus?

We walk down to the parking lot just as Jesse is pulling in and suddenly it occurs to me what he will think if he sees me with Sean. We aren't holding hands or anything, but his paranoid mind will go to the darkest place, for sure. He's been worried that I'll find a new boyfriend ever since I started school.

Sure enough, Jesse cranks the emergency brake into place and flies out of the car toward us.

"Who is this guy?" he shrieks.

Before I can respond, Sean steps in between us and puts his hand up. He's a pretty stocky, athletic guy with at least an inch or two of height on Jesse, but Jesse is enraged and throws a right hook straight into Sean's cheek.

I scream at him to get away just as my chemistry professor comes hustling toward us. He always parks in this lot and he saw the whole thing. Professor Currie hollers at Jesse and, thankfully, that's the end of it. He turns around and heads to his car, slams the door, and squeals out of the parking lot.

I'm going to throw up.

Sean's face is turning bright red, Professor Currie is looking at both of us in shock, and I am flush with shame. Sean swears he's just fine, and I thank them both for helping me before I lock my car and head back to my dorm. So much for reinventing myself. My worlds just collided.

––––––––––

I take a third job as an assistant in a family planning clinic over the summer and move in with Chris, who has graduated and is working as a social worker in a group home. I learn to run urine tests and work the centrifuge for blood samples. I counsel patients about birth control and STDs and assist during abortions and vasectomies. I have figured out how to use my ability to anticipate someone's needs and meet them without getting emotionally involved. I am empathetic and efficient, comforting and kind, and altogether uninvested in the outcome once they leave the clinic. I am good at my job and not responsible for anyone but myself.

Katy, on the other hand, is miserable. She drops out of school completely and Dallas kicks her out of the house. Mom calls me, frantic, saying Katy is gone—has she called me? I can feel the skin on my face stiffen as my jaw sets. No.

I love sharing the apartment with Chris because he works nights and has a cat named Xanadu, and we can live together without being in each other's faces all the time. This is my dream scenario—being an adult but still part of a family. Nobody needs me to take care of them except the patients I see and my cat, Marley.

After Katy leaves, Mom calls me almost every day to check in. One day she says she heard from someone that Katy is in Portland with a group of kids who are troublemakers. Mom wants to know if I've seen them.

"I haven't been looking," I snort. But a few days later, after nearly a solid week of rain, Katy calls me.

"Hey, Sissy. Did you hear Dallas kicked me out? I can't go back there. I won't. I've been staying in Portland with some friends, but we don't have a place so we've been on the street, but it's so wet. Most of them went home, but I can't and I'm cold and hungry. Can I come see you?" Her voice is raspy from smoking and shaky with emotion. The fact that she still calls me "Sissy" tugs at me.

I don't want to tell Chris. He will be so angry with me. He will mock me for saving her again, but my heart melts. I love her. I can't leave her on the street.

By the time I get downtown, the entire city is grey and slick. She is in Pioneer Courthouse Square, which, on a sunny day, is flecked with people eating lunch and basking in the sun. Today it is empty. Even the bums are huddled in the doorway of the courthouse to stay dry, but Katy sits on the soaked, red brick steps in defeat.

I slow down and reach across to heave the passenger door of my car open and her face lights up. She pops over to the sidewalk and when she gets in the car, she stinks of weed and sour sweat. I do my best not to recoil because she is beaming. It has been a long time since we saw each other.

In our kitchen with the scuttling silverfish, I make her a box of macaroni and cheese with frozen peas while she showers. When she gets out, she eats the whole thing. I tuck her into bed with Marley and head to work. When I get home around midnight, she hasn't moved, so I tuck the spaghetti and breadsticks I brought her into the fridge and tell Chris not to eat them. He grunts at me from his bedroom and shakes his head with a sarcastic smile. I know. I'm a sucker. But tomorrow, I'm calling Mom and telling her Katy's here, and we'll come up with a plan. Maybe Daddy will take her back if she promises to go to school. I don't know. I haven't talked to him much since he got remarried to the woman with three daughters that he was cheating on Susan with.

I stretch out on the couch to get some sleep before I head to the vet clinic. I'll go straight from there to my first class at 8:00 and then come back and check on Katy. Maybe by then I'll have put together a convincing speech because she sure as hell can't stay here.

It turns out I don't have to work on the speech at all. By the time I get home, she is gone along with my change jar and most of my cheap costume jewelry. Shit.

Chris was right. I wasn't doing Katy any favors by always solving her problems for her. I thought about how it must feel to be her, alone and scared, getting shuttled back and forth between Mom and Daddy. I wonder if she's angry with me for leaving her behind when I went to school or if she understood why I had to. I started fixing things for her as much for her own good as for mine. The fact is, not only did I love her and want her to be safe and happy, but I also didn't want to have to watch her suffer, and I felt good when I could solve a problem she had. I didn't have to see her suffer if I wrapped her in warm, soft blankets and hugged her tightly, but that didn't mean she wasn't suffering. Maybe what I was really doing was setting her up to fail. I thought I was mothering her, but since I didn't really know how to do that, maybe I was just making things worse by not letting her learn how to take care of her own problems or finding an adult who was capable of doing the things I couldn't do for her. I basically abandoned her when I left, as though someone would step up and fill the vacuum.

Book Two:

The Spiral

1996-2010

Revelations

Susan and I are lying on the double beds, recovering from the rough crossing. The trip from Seattle to Victoria on the Clipper was choppy, as it often is in spring. The bonus of crossing in the spring is that you can sometimes see whales and, at one point in the journey, the captain of the catamaran stopped the ship and announced that there was an entire pod of orcas in front of us.

I shook Susan awake and we made our way with the throngs of people to the front of the boat, staggering and holding on to the rails and laughing. We found spots along the side and stood speechless, watching the spectacular show the mothers and babies put on for us, tails slapping, breaching, spouting.

When the whales moved on at last, the ship picked up speed and bounced over the waves for another hour before we hit land. We headed straight to the hotel to lie down for a while and get our shore legs back.

Now, Susan is propped up on a mountain of pillows and I am sprawled on my back, one foot grounded firmly on the floor to combat the feeling that I am still rising and falling with the motion of the sea. I make the mistake of closing my eyes and bile rises in my throat.

I don't know how I got to the room at the back of the house or why. I was terrified of that shadowy space. I wouldn't dare go there on my own. Dark, homemade curtains were pulled across the window at the back of the room. Always pulled closed except for a slim triangular gap at the bottom where the corners didn't quite meet. I couldn't see anything through it but a dismal scrap of light and the mesh of the screen, but I focused on that light because it was the only light in the room. There was a mattress on the floor. Everything dark, navy sheets, clutter against the back wall, comic books, records, papers.

Shame. Thin mattress beneath my back on the floor, fingers pushing into me below my belly. Why am I here? I can't move or scream or say anything.

I sit up and take a ragged breath. Susan's eyes widen and she cocks her head.

"Oh God. Oh God. It happened to me, too." I can't move or breathe or think. The scene pulses in my mind.

Susan pushes herself up off of her bed and sits with me, her hand on my back.

"Katy. Her journal. The one she let you and Dad find. Where she said she was molested. She was right, of course she was right, but I mean, I just remembered. It was Clayton. At Jan's house. She was right. And he did it to me. Why didn't I stop it? Why didn't I tell someone? Why didn't I remember it?"

Wispy images groove and bend at the edges of my memory. There are great black holes in time where I have no recollection of anything positive or negative, no intelligible timelines.

But right now, I can see that bedroom with absolute clarity. I remember Clayton and his siblings, Shawna and Stevie. I haven't thought about them in years. My stomach rolls with the images as they push in to my consciousness. Stevie was a year younger than I was, but taller and stringy. He had oily hair that was too long and he was the kind of kid who pulled the legs off of spiders for sport. Jan, his mom, had a special tone of voice for him, shrill and sharp and full of points like his face. She sat at the linoleum-covered kitchen table, cotton-candy hair dyed purply-black and piled in a high beehive, snapping her gum and talking on the phone.

Shawna was the golden child and her mother's favorite. After Clayton was done with me, he would send me up to her room where I sat on the end of her bed, and we listened to "One Tin Soldier" by Coven on the record player in her room. I tried my best to imitate her voice as she taught me all the words, wailing on the highest notes, but she told me I was trying too hard. She made me sing it over and over again, and every time she mocked me, critiqued my voice, found something that I had to fix. I hated her, and I wanted to stay in her room forever. That light, bright room with its own pink Princess phone where I could just keep trying to get it right.

I jump up off the bed and dash to the bathroom to puke. Katy knew.

She never forgot. What must she have thought of me, when I didn't protect her from Clayton? What went through her mind as she and I were both molested, and I did nothing? I said nothing. I failed her.

———————

I graduated from college two years ago and moved to Seattle with Sean. We got married in 1994, and this trip is a fun girls' weekend with Susan. She and I are still really close—in fact, she was my matron of honor in our wedding—and this is supposed to be a grown-up adventure for the two of us. All weekend, I am distracted by the question of why this memory came up now, but I finally decide it's because I'm with Susan. Even though I started out hating her when she first married Daddy, she just kept showing up for me, supporting me, loving me. Now she is my closest friend.

I remember the first summer we lived in Wyoming. All of us were at Safeway picking up supplies for a Labor Day barbecue with the neighbors, and Daddy told me to go get some soda. I asked if we could have something besides diet soda, and I must have said it in a rude way because he grabbed me by the elbow and stuck his face in mine and hissed.

"Don't get sassy with me, young lady. You'll get what I tell you to get and you'll like it."

He didn't hurt me but I started crying loud, uncontrollable, hiccupping sobs, and once I started, there was no stopping. Susan put her arm around my shoulder and steered me down a different aisle, away from Daddy. She sat down in the middle of the cereal aisle with her back against the shelf and patted the floor next to her. I was paralyzed. If Daddy saw us, he would be furious that she was making a scene.

I finally sat down next to her, and she pulled me close.

"This must be so hard for you, Kari. To be in this new place with a new family, missing your mom and anxious about a new school. Want to talk about it?"

I remember thinking that there were so many things about Susan that were crazy. She wasn't afraid of Daddy like Mom was, and she was in charge of a lot of things in the house, like the backyard project. She did most of the cooking and cleaning like Mom, but she and Daddy decided things together most of the time. She talked back to him a lot, and sometimes it made Chris and me nervous because Daddy hated it when people disagreed with him. I couldn't believe she was so brave. Maybe it's because she was a single mother for so many years.

I wasn't sure what to do besides just lean in to her and keep crying until I was done. I had no idea where to start, and I wasn't sure I could trust her yet. But things are different now. Now, I know I can trust her. She has had my back from the beginning. I guess that's why my brain figured it was safe to remember.

Several months after this trip, I begin to struggle with anxiety. For some reason, my mind always goes to the worst-case scenario, which is really challenging given that Sean travels a lot for his work as a sales rep for Microsoft. Every time he leaves for the airport, I get a panicky feeling in my stomach and imagine his plane going down in flames. I hate that. I try to slam the door on that thought before it fully forms in my head because there is a part of me that believes that thinking it will make it so. There is another part of my mind that is horrified that I can even go there.

Every time I get sick, I start to wonder what it would be like to have cancer. I finally go to see a doctor because I have intermittent pain in my chest, and he rolls his eyes and tells me I am having panic attacks. He writes me a prescription for Xanax, which pisses me off. It's not all in my head. I'm strong, resilient, formidable. If I have chest pains, it must mean there is something really wrong.

I keep coming back to the same doctor until he agrees to run a series of tests on me. I lie and tell him I'm taking the Xanax, and it's not helping. I haven't even filled the prescription because I'm an OR tech, and there's no way I'm going to operate on other people while I'm doped up. He believes me and orders a bunch of blood tests and an EKG and tells me I'll have to wear a Holter monitor for 36 hours to track my heart activity. The only thing the test shows is that I have a heart murmur and mitral valve prolapse, and I grab on to those explanations like a life ring in the ocean. See? I'm not crazy.

I try not to let fear get the best of me, and for a while, it works. I believe that I've solved the mystery and, even though I don't take any medications for the heart issues, it seems like simply knowing about them is enough to make them stop almost completely.

Resistance

"You're wasting two perfectly good grandparents, here!" my father-in-law roars. He is sitting on the couch next to Sean's mom, and she looks almost as uncomfortable as I feel.

"Paul! Stop that." She clucks her tongue at him and lightly smacks his thigh in reproach, but I can tell she's conflicted. Sean and I have been married for nearly five years, and there is no sign of pregnancy. We just bought our first house, and I think they thought that's what we were waiting for—that we would finally start a family. The house is a split-level, three bedroom built in the 1970s with a huge, beautiful backyard. It's on a quiet cul-de-sac and close to schools, and his parents are sitting in our new living room simultaneously proud of us for doing such a grown-up thing and anxious to hear that this means we're having a baby. I wonder what they would think if they knew I had an abortion in high school. They would probably hate me.

"I'm kidding." Paul's eyes lock onto mine.

I want to look away, but I know better. If I show any weakness, he'll pounce. It's a game we've played since we first met and realized how diametrically opposed we are. He is a cattle farmer with conservative Republican values, and I am a vegetarian who put herself through college counseling women who were seeking abortions. My heroes are Gloria Steinem and Gandhi, and he looks up to Newt Gingrich and God.

"But, really," he leans in and softens his voice, "at some point, we will be too old to babysit and entertain grandchildren. We are in the prime of our lives right now with lots of free time and energy, so if you're going to have babies, this is the perfect time."

I want to throw up. I am *not* having children. I love my life. I love not being responsible for anyone but me. I am finally free of taking care of Mom or Katy or anyone else, and I'm not going back. Plus, with the recent revelation of just how badly I fucked up taking care of Katy, there is no way I'm going to try that again. I'm not built for mothering—giving it or receiving it.

My relationship with motherhood is complicated. As a child, I rarely felt as though I had enough mothering, and I was obsessed with finding it for myself and for Katy. Somehow, I knew that it was a vital part of survival. At some point, I decided that Mom needed mothering, too, and I filled my own need for nurturing by becoming the nurturer. In a not-altogether conscious way, I chose the role of mother as a way to get mothering for all of us, but it became clear to me pretty quickly that I wasn't doing it right, and I began resenting everything that motherhood stood for.

In my own attempts to fix things for Katy and Mom, I was fully aware that I was making shit up as I went. I felt completely incompetent and unprepared, fueled by fear more than anything, and I came to believe that all mothers were flying by the seat of their pants. And still, I craved it, I saw it as one of the most important things a human could have. I wanted it more than anything for myself. I did it for Katy because I was certain she wouldn't survive without it. And I did it for Mom because I thought I could somehow remind her what to do and how to do it.

Despite my desperate desire for mothering, when I was given opportunities to be taken care of, I struggled to trust it. I had seen how mothering could be there one minute and gone the next. I pushed against Mom's occasional attempts to care for me as if to test her resolve, and eventually, she just let me push her away entirely. When Susan stepped in to help, like the time I woke her up in the middle of the night because I had fallen out of the top bunk and gouged my head on the corner of the desk, it felt surreal. She didn't yell at me or complain—she simply led me to her bathroom and gently washed the blood away with hydrogen peroxide, examined the gash in my head, and patched it up gently. I still remember how soft and warm her hands were and how we joked that I might have a blonde streak in my hair for the summer from the peroxide, but maybe because it was midnight or because I was fiercely loyal to my mom, I never really let myself believe that I could be mothered by Susan, and so I didn't let it happen.

And yet, mothering is in my DNA. For all of my anger toward Mom for not being the kind of mother I thought she should be, she had a reputation for taking care of other people. She married a man who told her he had terminal cancer in order to make the remaining years of his life comfortable. She was often on the phone with girlfriends who struggled with defiant children or angry husbands or women who had just lost a job. She was a waitress with a loyal following because she remembered just how people liked their coffee and always made sure they had enough water and they knew she really wanted them to have a good experience. Her real estate practice was focused on "women in transition," serving those who were newly divorced or widowed or were in need of honest advice. She was as much social worker as listing agent. Her sisters are all nurturing, caring, empathetic souls who will give you the shirt off their back, no questions asked. It's a family tradition to take care of other people.

But as I got older and more tired and increasingly resentful, I decided mothering was something to be avoided. I became actively disdainful of anyone who tried to mother me. I armored myself by telling myself I didn't need it anymore; I wasn't weak enough to need it. My motivations to have an abortion at 17 were many, but one of the most visceral reactions I had when I realized I was pregnant was horror at the thought that I would never break free of mothering if I continued the pregnancy. I would be mothering Jesse and the baby indefinitely.

My avoidance of mothering has worked for years. I aligned myself with Chris, who didn't need me to mother him. I finally broke up with Jesse and began dating Sean, whose mother did her job just fine. I actively chose jobs that put me in roles where I took care of others—tutoring, medical assisting, counseling—but I rationalized those things because they were transactional and not survival-based. None of the people I helped would ever mistake me for their mother, but maybe I was fulfilling my genetic mothering destiny by finding a different way to take care of people without actually being a mother. I could act that way without all the emotional weight or responsibility it entailed.

I'm not telling Sean's dad any of this, though. I already feel like the outcast in this family. Sean, whose grandparents all lived within a mile of the farmhouse where he grew up, whose parents have been married since they were teenagers, whose siblings all went to college like they were sup-posed to and have good jobs with benefits, who have epitomized the Nor-man Rockwell experience by spending every single Christmas together in the same house and taking vacations together and talking on the phone every Sunday night, is normal. Sean's parents unfortunately know of my dad because they live in Lebanon and when he and Susan got divorced, it was the talk of the town that Daddy had cheated on her with a much younger woman. They know my mom is on her third husband, having finally ditched Dallas after five horrid years in his Mountain Man cabin. That is enough. They don't need to know any more. I love them and I desperately want to fit in with his family, but I'm not having kids to make them happy.

I started dating Sean in college because he was unlike anyone I had ever met. He was smart, self-assured, and completely uninhibited. Being around him was fun, and I was just beginning to learn what that was like. Even though he was a year older than I was, he was in no hurry to grow up and he always believed things would work out if you just gave them time. And I never had to fix anything for him. He even took a punch to the face for me.

I told him more than once that I was never having kids because I wanted to be completely up-front with him. I was also determined to pay my own way for everything. I bought my own movie tickets, offered to drive half the time, took him out to brunch or dinner to repay him taking me out. I was not going to be beholden to anyone. I saw how hard it was for Mom after Daddy left, and there was no way I was going to be dependent on anyone else for my survival.

When we got our first apartment, I paid half the rent. When he con-tinued to get pay raises and I didn't, I told him we couldn't move because I couldn't afford it. For the first few years we were married, I refused to have a joint bank account because I wanted to be able to keep track of all the money I had. I needed to know that if he left me, I could survive on my own. And "on my own" doesn't include kids.

Katy has moved on too. She finally got her GED and moved back to Salem with Mom. She met a lovely, sweet boy named Isaiah, and they got married in a traditional Vietnamese ceremony that was odd and quirky and perfectly Katy. The two of them work in a ceramics shop making delicate Christmas ornaments for Margaret Furlong, and I'm so glad. Maybe I did the right thing by distancing myself and letting her figure some stuff out on her own. She had some scary years, and she and Mom have had some massive issues, but they seem to be in a good place now. Mom is remarried to Ken, a real estate agent she met in Salem, and he's a total sweetheart—the polar opposite of Mountain Man Dallas, who is still living in that nasty cabin in the woods with all his animal pelts and woodstove.

Two Steps Forward...

A few days before Thanksgiving, Katy calls early in the morning to say that her husband is dead. She found sweet, sweet Isaiah hanging from the ceiling in their living room. Will I come? Sean and I pack furiously. I call work to tell them I won't be in for a while. We race to Oregon as fast as we can, but the traffic is awful, thanks to the upcoming holiday. We finally make it to Mom's house in Salem, and I don't even wait for Sean to turn the engine off before I sprint to the door and fling it open and wrap Katy in my arms. I have a desperate ache in me, like a magnet trying to draw the pain and shock out of her body and in to mine, but it isn't working. All I can do is stand there and hold her as she shakes. I can't make a joke or play a game to fix this.

Mom and Katy argue about where she will sleep. Katy doesn't want to leave their little house empty, but Mom says Katy can't go back there. Katy says she feels Isaiah there, that she has to go back, but she doesn't want to be alone, so I offer to go with her. Walking in to the dark, incense-scented living room, I bite my lips closed and try to still the frantic racing of my heart. She lies down on the couch, and I climb behind her, curling my body around hers to keep her warm and still her quaking. After a while, she falls asleep, and so do I.

A few weeks after we come home, it is time to pack for Christmas. Sean's sister and Sean and I will load her car with gifts and bags and head to Oregon to spend the week with his family. Sean comes in to the bedroom to ask if we have more tape and finds me hiding beneath the covers, an open suitcase on the foot of the bed. He stops midsentence and comes to sit next to me.

"You okay, babe?"

I whimper but I really can't speak. My heart is pounding, my breath comes in short puffs when I remember to breathe, my head is spinning.

"What do you need?"

Words explode from my lips without ever forming in my head. "I want someone to take care of me."

I am horrified. I want to take it back. Why did I say that? What does it even mean? I shove the covers back and sit up, ashamed. Because it's true. I don't want to be an adult and make important decisions, pay bills, take care of everything when he travels. I don't want to admit that I can't fix things the way they should be fixed. I'm no good at it. Maybe I never was. But it's all I've done my whole life. I can't stop now.

"I mean, I'm just sad. Poor Katy. I can't help her. I can't make it better. And now it's Christmas and I just hate to see her like this. It's okay. I'll be all right. Maybe I'll go take a hot shower and finish packing. You should run to Target and get more tape so we can finish wrapping everything."

––––––––––

I have a twisted relationship with a massage therapist. He brutalizes me, I suffer through it, and at the end of 50 minutes, I shower praise on him as though he were the second coming of chocolate.

I lie on my back, flannel sheet draped over me, heated mattress beneath. This is the only pleasant part of this ritual. I close my eyes and listen for the squelch of the lotion in his hands that signals the start of my torture. Light pressure begins at the base of my skull and moves down the side of my neck, slowly making the curve to my shoulders. I think of my great grandmother kneading dough for pierogies, warming it with the soft touch of her hands, smoothing the surface, stretching the elastic dough slowly and gently.

But he finds a ridge, a cord of muscle fibers that have braided themselves together to hold a deposit of stress. His fingertips press in, separating the strands of muscle, vibrating deeper and deeper as my muscles tense and push back in defense. His fingers slip off into the soft tissue beside it, and he tries again. He finds the length of tightness, and this time I remember to breathe, drop my diaphragm down and out, and deliver oxygen to my muscles. I try to imagine the fibers loosening up and parting in spite of the pain. This is so counterintuitive. I want to ask him to ease up but I can't speak. I have convinced myself that the bruising comes when I indulge my instinct to resist and tense against his push.

While I am lying on my stomach, my face presses into the cradle scented with lavender. He finds the area between my spine and shoulder blade and plays piano there for a while. A spark of red pain lights its way down my arm and again, I forget to breathe. He digs his elbow into the gravelly tissue and pulses it slowly, pushing at the muscles to break apart the toughness there, and I try to focus on breathing in and out, pushing rich blood through the traffic jam of knots.

He grunts as he hits a particularly dense spot. This is hard work, I know. My toes curl as I try to find one place on my body that I can tense up so that the others can let go. I imagine him walking me to the door later and saying, *Man, you have the tightest/worst/most messed-up muscles I've ever seen!* I want to believe that my pain tolerance is higher than anyone else's and that his hands and elbows are sore after he is done with me. I want to be his toughest client in every sense of the word.

I want him to comment on my deep breathing and my ability to take the pain. I want him to acknowledge that I never ask him to let up or take it easy. He never does.

Instead, he smiles and leads me to the glass of water he poured for me. He says he hopes he was helpful and will I be there next week. I will. Even though I will feel bruised and battered for the next two days, there is something compelling about proving to myself that I can take it—that without pain, there is no gain.

Building a Family

These days, I feel a strange pull to create a family, and it is terrifying. Despite my pledge that I will never be responsible for another child and my absolute determination to not fail anyone like I failed Katy and Cameron, the feeling that our lives are empty without children becomes more and more present. I know Sean wants children, but he has never pushed the idea. We are young and building our careers, paying off student loans, spending our weekends working in the yard, and going out with friends. But all of a sudden, I feel like that's not enough.

One Sunday morning as we lie in bed slowly waking up, I roll over and curl myself into the side of his body. I push my face right up to the side of his head and whisper cautiously, "I think I want to have a baby."

To his credit, he doesn't laugh or move quickly or scream, "I TOLD you so!" He just reaches down to squeeze my hand and whispers back, "Cool. Me too."

———

I've been on the pill for nearly twelve years so I'm not entirely sure how long it will take to get pregnant, but apparently, I needn't have worried. The first month I stop taking my pills, I get pregnant.

As soon as Sean and I are done celebrating, I begin to think about what this child's family will look like. I had thought I had time to ruminate on all of those things, but apparently, I have less time than I realized. I am not particularly close to Mom or Dad, and I haven't been for years. In my quest to distance myself from any family drama, I've firmly aligned myself with Sean's "normal" family, to the point where I barely see my folks for holidays and never stay at either of their houses when we come to town. I think about how to tell them that we're having a baby, and, although I want it to be a sweet, loving moment, the fact is, I am still so angry with both of them that I don't know whether I can pull that off or not.

Over the years, despite the sordid stories I heard from Susan and Mom about Daddy's behavior, I never bothered to confront him because I knew what happened when you asked for the truth in my family—you ended up feeling like you had done something wrong or you were crazy. Instead, I distanced myself. As for Mom, she had a way of changing the subject by making it all about her, like the time I mustered up the courage to tell her that I remembered Clayton molesting me. I wanted to give her some idea of what Katy must have been going through all those years— living with that knowledge on her own, little shoulders. I had hoped it would give her compassion for Katy and help Mom understand why Katy acted the way she did. I stood in my bedroom and gazed out the window to the trees in the yard and called her. We exchanged pleasantries and then I told her I needed to tell her something that might help explain some of those really hard years back in Lincoln City. She got quiet, and when I was done talking, she got angry.

"You know, all I ever wanted was to have a houseful of kids and be a mom. I was really upset when the doctor told me I couldn't have any more babies. But then we adopted Katy, and I thought it was God's blessing. His plan was for me to provide a loving home for children who wouldn't otherwise have one, so I got over my sadness and embraced that plan. And then your dad ruined it all, and I had to go out and work."

"Okay, Mom, but I'm saying—Katy was right. And I feel so guilty! Clayton molested me too, and I never told anyone. Why didn't I tell anyone?"

"I'm saying, that if your father and I hadn't gotten a divorce, it never would have happened. That's what I'm saying. So, I guess he ruined your life, too."

In that moment, I wrestled with the realization that this was probably something incredibly painful for her to hear—that she might carry some guilt about having placed us in that situation in the first place—and with the need I had to have her absolve me, to tell me that it wasn't my fault. Ultimately, my need won out. She was the mother, I rationalized. It was her job to listen to me, acknowledge my pain, and comfort me, and her inability to do any of that simply widened the chasm between us. She had disappointed me again, and I resigned myself to believing that she could never be the mom I needed her to be.

Just like I had with Jesse, I took the coward's way out. Rather than continuing to make an effort to resolve things with Mom or Dad or cutting them off completely, I simply hung out in some superficial space of cordial visits a few times a year where we talked about work and the weather and had a nice meal. Formal disengagement would have required an honest conversation and, most likely, a nasty fight, or it would have led me back to that place where I felt like my view of the world was so skewed that I must be nuts. I didn't want any of that, so I pretended everything was fine and so did they.

But now that I am having a baby, I feel like I have a decision to make about whether or not I'm going to let my parents be a real part of this child's life. I start to really think about the life I want to give to our baby. I recall family Christmases before the divorce, smack in the middle of a tornado of cousins, aunts, uncles, and grandparents, torn tissue and ribbons and smiles all around. I remember that allies don't always come in the form we expect them to and, regardless of how badly I want to be the one my child comes to when she needs help, it dawns on me that I may not be the one she chooses. God knows I never chose either one of my parents to confide in. How could I have ever predicted that Susan would be my best friend and confidante?

I decide that I want to give our baby the biggest, most loving family in the history of the world. I want her to know her grandparents and aunts and uncles and cousins. I want her to hear their stories and see their hilarious antics. I want her to stand in the center of a room full of her people and feel loved and protected and cherished. I start with Dad.

My heart softens as I recall some of my favorite moments with him: playing "Heart and Soul" on the piano, hiking in the mountains on a sunny day, listening to him play Pete Seeger tunes on the banjo. Over the years, I had let myself forget how safe I felt with him as a kid most of the time, how much I craved his attention and love, how much I wanted him to be proud of me.

The problem is, I don't really know how to go about engaging in a relationship with him. I will have to steel myself for this conversation, this decision to really let him in to my life. I will have to confront him with all the accusations Mom and Susan made and force him to answer for them, right? Maybe not. Gradually, it begins to dawn on me that there is really nothing he can say to defend himself. Can I actually imagine a scenario where he'll say, "Oh, I cheated on your mom because _____" and I can nod my head and say, "Oh, now I get it. Okay"? Can I come up with any plausible explanation for some of the decisions he made as a parent? Is there anything that will make me think, *Yep, I totally would have done the same thing*?

Instead, I ask myself a different question, one that feels more important to me today, as an adult. *Had any of the things he did been motivated by malice or hatred for me or my siblings or even Mom? Had he made those choices out of an honest desire to hurt any of us?*

I know the answer is no, and I still wrestle with these thoughts for a long time. I go back and forth between the desire to punish him—or at least have him punished—for his actions, and shutting the door on all of it and starting over. I finally decide that it isn't my job to make him pay for things he did to someone else—or for any of his mistakes, for that matter. There's something that bothers me about this—like it's taking the easy way out again by not having the hard conversations and ultimately, it's letting him off the hook—but maybe the hardest part is simply acknowledging that this man, who was my hero for so many years, the person I most wanted to please, is actually human. Maybe I need to let him down off that pedestal and try to relate to him human being to human being.

I call to tell him I'm pregnant.

"...and I wanted to say that I would like us to start over. No revisiting past issues. We are both adults, and I'm going to make my own choices and let you make yours without judgment. I love and respect you, and I want the same treatment from you. I hope we can find a way to just love and support each other, and I want you to be part of my child's life. You have no power over me anymore and while I want you to be proud of me, I don't need you to be. I just need you to love me and this baby."

I am shaking. I've never talked to my Dad like this. I have rarely ever set boundaries like this. It isn't the most sentimental speech ever, but Dad chokes up.

"You got it, kiddo. I'm excited for you two. You're going to make terrific parents."

———————

Pregnant, I move through the world with this sense that the baby inside me is mine. Not in the sense that she shares my DNA, but in the sense that she belongs to me. I had purposefully set out to get pregnant, she was housed in my belly, and I was constantly reminded that everything I did impacted her tiny, developing self in a big way.

"Get enough sleep."

"No soft cheeses."

"No caffeine or alcohol."

But the truth is, even before I knew I was pregnant, this ball of cells was busy dividing over and over again, creating a protective shell around itself. Even before I peed on that stick, my daughter had formed her first layer of defense—a shield against the world.

Now that I know, I feel like I am the creator, and she is my lump of clay. I pick through the list of our traits like a bowl of cocktail nuts in my mind, gently pushing aside the too-common peanuts and the over-large Brazil nuts, concocting the perfect mix of Sean and me.

Please let her teeth be naturally straight like his. Let her have my eyesight. It would be awesome if she had his strategic mind and my compassionate heart.

I am not even aware of the fact that her strongest biological imperative from this moment forward is to separate, differentiate, become an individual, despite the fact that she tries to warn me. In the middle of the second trimester, she shimmies and shakes, dancing and cavorting inside me, pushing against my flesh in a gymnastics routine of her own design. No matter that I am trying to sleep. She is making herself known. Within a few weeks, she begins demanding fresh pineapple and German pancakes. The burning in my gut is unlike anything I have ever known, and I develop a pack-a-day Tums habit.

But I still think of her as mine, like some pesky appendage that won't quite do what I ask it to, but will eventually.

I go into labor with her sitting posterior in my womb, her head pressed firmly up against my tailbone. While I writhe in back labor, my doctor stands on the left and a nurse stands on the right, flanking my belly and kneading it like so much bread dough, pushing to maneuver her into a position where she can be safely delivered. With each subsequent contraction, she calmly somersaults herself right back to where she had been before. Tenacious and precise, this little girl is delivered in the posterior position after 40 hours of labor. Erin arrives on her due date after we all finally give up trying to make her do what we think is best.

Still, I persist with the notion that she is mine. She looks exactly how I had on the day I was born—skinny and long with feathery black hair and olive skin. When I compare her with my baby photo, the similarities are astonishing.

For weeks after she is born, I feel phantom kicks in my belly. Even as I care for her in every way, I mourn the loss of our physical union and the ease with which I could sustain her when I was pregnant. I begin to realize that motherhood is an exercise in opposites, the crashing together of the two most profound human emotions—love and fear. As much as I had felt those things with Katy, I was not prepared for the intensity of emotion I experienced with Erin. The pure, golden light of mother-love is quickly tainted by the crushing responsibility I feel. The sudden dawning that I am not prepared to bear the weight of each and every decision made on behalf of this human being is accompanied by the solid weight of warmth wrapped in a flannel blanket in my arms and the joy I feel at calling her daughter. I want to spend every second gazing down at her, consumed by the sight and smell and heft of her. But that adoration is tinged with pangs of absolute terror every time I hold her, touch her, look at her ruddy cheeks or her tiny toes. That explosive burst of love exists side by side with the metallic ache of fear, the joy of having this thing that I love so much and the possibility that I will one day fail her.

Increasingly, Erin asserts herself as I live in the limbo between celebrating and lamenting her fierce independence. I struggle to put limits on her as much out of fear for her physical safety as well as some fuzzy notion of what a mother is supposed to look like. All the while, I proudly recognize myself in her: her sense of priorities, her stubborn determination to conquer any challenge she deems worthy of her attention. I identify with her again and again, blurring the line between the two of us as surely as if I am reattaching the umbilical cord.

I have the solid notion that she is a part of me, like one of the rays of a sea star, but I am so wrong. She is her own person, and she fights to show me that again and again. I begin to realize that my notion of motherhood revolves around survival and protection, controlling every variable to produce the outcome I want. I am increasingly unable to enjoy the quiet moments with her and the awe of watching her explore her world because I am terrified to fail her, to lose her. My mothering becomes frantic and desperate, like it had been with Katy. My very existence and worth rests on how well I can do this job, on whether I can avoid the same mistakes I made with my sister.

In my mind, the moment I lost control as a kid was when Mom went to work. I had never had any say in what happened with Cameron, but when I assumed the role of mother to Katy in Mom's absence, things fell apart. The fact was, I had no business doing any of that, but I had built my entire identity around it. Now I am a mother for real. I believe that if I just keep a tidy house, put healthy, homemade meals on the table three times a day, read to Erin and enable Sean to indulge his dreams, my family will stay together forever. I am determined that this house will not be a house of cards.

One day while Erin is napping, I busy myself cleaning out the closet in the guest room and come across a letter Daddy wrote to me when I graduated from high school. I can't believe how long ago that feels. Most of it is predictable philosophical parenting advice, assuring me that I can be whatever I want to be, pleading with me to make good choices in college, but I am struck by the last paragraph.

> …you have a very obvious desire to be around other people and seek out people who need help. While that is a laudable thing to do, please remember that the absolute best help you can give another is to require them to help themselves— that you do them no favors by allowing them to lean on you and your help. Your sensitivity is a very precious thing and I hope you retain it all your life. Mostly, I hope that you use it with wisdom and not just emotion—for emotion you have

always had in abundance, too. Maybe someday you will find this letter and it will make more sense than it does now. I love you, Dad

I don't even remember reading this that day. I don't know that it would have made any sense to me then. I am shocked that this is the kind of insight my Dad had into me all those years ago and I wonder what else he knew that he never talked about.

Collapse

I have two little girls now. Erin is five and her little sister, Lauren, is two. We moved to a bigger house on two acres on a quiet cul-de-sac, and I haven't had a paying job since Erin was born. I sometimes feel guilty about that, since I spent so much money and time getting my college degrees and I had so much ambition, but the fact is, Sean travels a great deal for work and I refuse to let anyone else raise my children. He's still at Microsoft, and he's in charge of a partner program that takes him all over the world.

I plan on going back to work when the girls are in school, but Sean's parents are thrilled that I am a stay-at-home mom. They are sure to remind me how important it is that I am here for my girls. Mom is jealous, reminding me that that is the life she wanted, too, but didn't get, thanks to Dad, and I can't bring myself to respond when she talks about it.

Dad and I have become really close. Watching him get down on the floor to play dress-up with Erin and sing silly songs is one of the most healing things I can imagine. He treats my daughters with kindness and gives them the unconditional love I wanted from him as a child. They adore him and so do I.

But I am exhausted. In the past six months, I have changed nearly every light bulb in this house and washed the glass on the French doors and all the windows on the first floor inside and out. I have vacuumed every nook and cranny of the house to remove cobwebs, captured and released countless spiders from the girls' bedrooms, and shopped for, prepared, and cleaned up after a million meals. I have arranged for the new furnace to be installed, dealt with the insurance company when the septic tank failed, gone without running water for three days while it was repaired, and taken care of the yard. I have managed the health insurance, arranged doctor visits, found house and pet sitters when we leave town, and done four loads of laundry a week. I have driven to swimming lessons and gymnastics, changed diapers, read stories for hours every day, colored, sung, and rocked the girls to sleep. I have planned birthday parties and researched preschools. I have done dishes and swept floors and cleaned bathrooms and countertops and had the oil changed in the car.

The problem with most of the things I do on a daily basis is that nobody notices them unless they aren't done. Clean dishes in the cupboard and fresh towels in the linen closet are taken for granted because that's how it's supposed to be. It is expected that there will be food in the pantry and the cat's dish and that the lights will come on when someone flicks the switch. In Sean's work world, there are products—tangible things that he creates to prove his worth. True, the absence of a report might be felt, but maybe not as keenly as the lack of a clean towel when you step out of the shower soaking wet. This makes it a challenge to prioritize.

The things that everyone else relies on feel more important and more immediate than the things I could potentially do for myself. There are categories of caretaking that seem to define which things get done first, but in general those things are relentless and ongoing. And when something unexpected happens—a kid falls down and is bleeding or the toilet overflows—those things pile on top and the notion of doing something restorative or creating something new or just FUCKING SITTING DOWN QUIETLY TO STARE AT THE WALL seems impossible.

I have become so adept at anticipating the needs of others and meeting them that I have set myself up to be the one responsible for all things. My need for order and the ego boost that comes along with being the caretaker have boxed me into a corner, and to stop now and ask for help feels absurd, if not incredibly disruptive and unfair to everyone else. And I have done it to myself.

I am in crisis, and I got myself here by building my identity around being The Mother, the one who solves all problems and takes care of everyone, and the perverse thing is that every night when I go to bed I mentally catalogue all of the things I did for other people and pat myself on the back for it.

Most days, I can summon the energy to plod through oatmeal break-fasts and sunscreen applications and play dates in the park. I rarely succumb to TV-as-babysitter for the girls because I know they need me to be an active part of their lives. But as they get older, there are entire days when I want nothing more than to escape to my bedroom, close the door, and dive beneath the down comforter. I want to shut out the world and all its demands. I am astonished at how hard it is to just stay in the room with the girls playing Polly Pocket or reading *Bear Wants More* for the seventeenth time in one day.

But instead of giving me empathy for Mom, helping me understand why she simply couldn't do it all anymore, I blame her. I am angry that she laid down the mantle of motherhood and let me pick it up without protest. I am filled with rage that her memories of my childhood are populated with fun road trips and bonfires on the beach while mine are filled with the lack of her. I hate that she tells Erin and Lauren stories of pets and picnics and that she looks at me wide-eyed and denies it when I tell them about her using the wooden spoon on our bare bottoms when we were bad. She claims to have forgotten most of the things that I remember as frightening or sad and when I press, she gets angry and refuses to talk.

I begin most days with a wedge of anxiety lodged in my chest—what if I can't hold it together today? What if I fail my daughters?

"Many of your symptoms of anxiety—the sweaty palms, the racing heart, the nausea—result from your hypervigilance . . ."

My therapist's words reverberate in my head and make their way down into my bones where they resonate in a steady drum beat. I *am* hypervigilant—always on the lookout, alert for danger, never resting. That is me.

I stop listening to her words and turn the word hypervigilant over and over in my mind. I attach a kite string to it and sail it high above my head in the sky. It is my banner, my truth, my Self. Trailing my gaze up the string, I begin recounting the times in my life I've caught danger just before things spiraled out of control. I recall the occasions I've congratulated myself on my ability to notice that something wasn't quite right and swerve just in time to avoid disaster. I wonder how it can be a bad thing if it kept me safe for so long. In my head, hypervigilance looks like a brightly colored eye with a ten-thousand-foot view—scanning the world for potential threats.

But it *is* a bad thing, because it's destroying me. Somewhere along the way, I turned the corner from vigilant to vigilante. I am no longer holding the string. I have become the kite. Rather than simply paying attention, I now actively seek danger, look for harm like some twisted superhero. I create chaos just so that I can clean it up and prove that I'm strong, smart, capable, in control. I destroy ants with cannonballs because it makes me feel invincible.

––––––––––

The cars are lined up for morning drop-off—minivans, SUVs, a few Microsoft dads in their sports cars with eager kindergarten students strapped into their car seats. I drive past them all and park in the shade.

"Erin, get your school bag and your coat, please." I look back over my shoulder and wink at Lauren. Walking around to slide the van door open, I breathe deeply through widened nostrils and fill my chest to bursting like I learned in yoga. I exhale in a loud, "Hoooo," and drop my shoulders to relax the muscles in my neck.

I never drop Erin off in the car line. Her teachers smile as we swing the heavy classroom door open and make our way past children hanging coats and bags up on the hooks bearing their names. Erin makes her way to her cubby with a gait that makes her ponytail swing back and forth, and I bend down with Lauren on my hip to firmly kiss the top of her head, swallowing against the lump in my throat. Her friends greet her with smiles and hugs, and she squirms away from me, ready to giggle with her gang as they move toward the reading circle in a big, swirling mass.

I walk slowly back down the hallway, bouncing Lauren on my hip as I blink away tears.

"What shall we do today, just you and me, huh? Shall we do Play-Doh? Or finger painting? Too cold for the park, I think, sweetie pie, but we'll have some special time, just you and me."

She twists herself around to look back at the classroom and points.

She wants to go with her big sister. I kiss her warm cheek and snuggle her in tighter.

"Paintin'," she finally says as I strap her in to her car seat, and I nod in agreement. I feel awful for setting her up like this, but I have no intention of doing anything this afternoon but napping. I drive the three miles home just under the speed limit, sneaking glances in the mirror to see if she is falling asleep. I keep the music low and my speed steady and speak only when she forces me to. I feel guilty. I know I should take her home and play with her, give her the focused attention I promised, but I want to sleep. Sleeping makes the time go faster and I want it to be time to go pick Erin up from school.

I can't shake the panicky feeling that she is in danger. There is a prickly ball churning in my stomach, bumping up against the sides and sending shock waves of nerve pain through my body. I am jumpy, edgy. My clothes feel like sandpaper. Even after all the work I've done in therapy, I still can't shake the awful feeling I get when I drop her at school.

When I figure it out, I almost drive off the road into the ditch. Erin is five. She is in half-day kindergarten. This morning, I accidentally called her "Katy."

I have to protect her.

When we get home, Lauren and I do puzzles, read board books, finger-paint. She managed to stay awake during the drive home, and I'm struggling to keep it together. Living with this prickly ball makes my molars set together and my shoulders hunch up near my earlobes. I color inside the lines with incredible precision and watch the arms of the clock snail by until the moment I can justify scooping Lauren up and fastening her into the car seat for the trek back to school.

We get there too early. I spy through the tiny window in the classroom door and see Erin smiling as she bends over her work. She looks up to see me standing there and waves us in. Lauren squirms out of my arms and runs to join the other children for closing circle. I stand in the doorway for a beat and watch as Erin puts her arm protectively around her little sister. The lump in my throat grows.

On the way home, I spray her with questions like buckshot, soaking up every detail of her day without me. What did she do? Who did she play with? What songs did they sing? What is happening tomorrow?

I wonder how long I will watch her like this. Will there ever come a day when I can stop worrying that she will be molested or taken away?

———————

At some point, I crumble. For all of my frantic running around, taking care of things, I can't quiet the storm in my gut that says it's not enough. One morning I stand in the shower, shoulders hunched, unable to stop or even slow the torrent of tears flooding my face. After months of fighting to stay strong, the dam has broken and I can no longer hide. I haven't told Sean how depressed I am because I am afraid he will send me away to get help, and I can't bear to abandon the girls.

But it's more than that. I love Sean and I know that sharing my fears would make him feel trapped, or tricked. Nobody wants to hear me complain. And I have assured him over and over again with my actions that I am capable of holding up my part of this partnership. I can't admit now that I'm not up to the task.

My parents' voices echo in my head: *Get over it. Suck it up. It's really not that big a deal. You're so emotional! Calm down. Don't you know how lucky you are?*

In my head and my heart, I am eight years old again. I am that terrified kid who can't seem to see the world straight. Every person in my family has a different story about that tumultuous time. My eight-year-old brain saw things that Chris's eleven-year-old self didn't. I felt things that were entirely alien to him. How do I know what Mom told people about the sequence of events—Cameron leaving, the divorce, the remarriages, how everyone left town? How do I know that she and Dad didn't shape the narrative in their own way over and over again, design it to slide across the palate more easily (or stick in their throats, depending on what they needed from the person they were telling)?

What I do know is that the cloak of pain and longing that I donned during that time was so thick as to be impenetrable. As an eight-year-old whose family was exploding before her eyes, I was concerned with survival. It was losing my brother, and then my father, and finally, my mother, that cemented my view of the world as black and white, that dictated my future behavior would be inflexible and ruled by fear. I came to know deep in my bones, because I was never told any differently, that I was contingent, that I could be erased quickly and permanently from my family after one misstep. All the more frightening was the fact that, despite many attempts, I never learned what Cameron's misstep had been. He was not a biological child, but neither was Katy, and while she was in danger of erasure as well, she acted out more boldly and violently than Cameron ever had and she wasn't banished—at least not overtly. The years following that event were a minefield precisely because I didn't know the rules, but I still knew I had to follow them.

I became an extraordinarily compliant child. I stopped asking questions, partly because I was afraid everyone else knew something I didn't, but also because I was afraid that speaking out could be my undoing. I didn't challenge my parents, I accommodated them. I became adept at reading the needs of others and meeting those needs. I also tried my best to make myself indispensable. My simple equation was this: if I made everyone's lives easier, getting rid of me would make their lives harder.

That is still the standard I live by. If I fall apart now, Sean won't want me.

Sometimes as I drive home from the park or the swimming pool, I flinch at every intersection, imagining the driver coming toward me running the red light and slamming into the driver's side of the car. In my mind, I see us careening into the other lane, glass showering my hair and clothes, airbags deploying in clouds of dust. The girls are fine. It is just me that is crushed.

Other times, as I walk through the neighborhood lost in thought, I think about what it would be like to slip through a pile of wet leaves and mud and fall into the street, breaking bones or getting hit by a passing car.

As I hurry down the thickly carpeted steps to the main floor, I gasp as I imagine one foot sliding out from beneath me so I tumble end over end, landing in a heap on the hardwood floor below.

This is my mind's way of conjuring up a scenario where it is okay for me to ask for help. Nobody could deny that I would need taking care of if I were in the hospital with broken bones and cuts. Nobody could call me weak or fault me for resting and healing. Nobody would say I had deserted my children. They would understand.

Sean stands outside the shower, clean khakis and a button-down shirt tucked in tight. He has come to kiss me goodbye as he heads out for another long day. I can't see beyond the glass doors of the shower into another day so I slump down on the cobbled plastic of the shower floor, tuck my face into my hands, and sob.

He sits down on the edge of the adjacent tub and cocks his head. After a moment of silence, he stretches his arms out in offering.

I slide the door open and step out without shutting off the water.

He encloses me in his arms even as I pull back to avoid soaking his work shirt. Running his hands over my head, he asks, "What's going on?"

I spew forth details of weeks and months of agony and self-loathing and admit that I am barely hanging on. I want to die. I am so ashamed, but slowly I begin to realize that instead of anger, hatred, or disgust, Sean is simply holding me and stroking my wet hair.

"Why did you wait so long to tell me?"

"You have so much on your plate right now with work and the house and supporting all of us. I can't add to that."

"Then I will just get a bigger plate to hold it all. You are more important than work or the house." His response sends shock waves through my body.

I pour out my insecurities, terrified that I am destroying my place in this family as the cornerstone of this operation. I am certain that now that I have admitted my failings, I cannot be considered indispensable or worth keeping around.

Sean looks at me, genuinely puzzled. "I don't *need* you, babe. I haven't ever *need*ed you. I'm here because I want you."

His words slice through me. I'm sure I heard him wrong. It can't be true that he doesn't need me. I've worked long and hard to show him what a good wife and mother I can be. I have shown him in countless ways how much he needs me. What is he saying?

"I'm a pretty self-sufficient person. Pretty independent . . ."

HA! I want to scream. *HA! Who raises your children when you're away on business for days or weeks? Who feeds them, shops for them, takes them to music class?* My internal tirade is interrupted as he sits and pulls me onto his lap.

"I'm not here because I need you. I'm here because I want you. I always have. That will last a lot longer than need. Need is transactional. Want is about you and me. But you have to trust me and share things with me. You have to let me be a full partner in this relationship."

I hear a voice in my head saying that the currency exchange of need to want is like dollars to Colombian pesos. They might both be valuable to some extent, but it takes three thousand pesos to make a dollar, so in my hand, want might look like a lot, but it's really just a pile of paper that doesn't add up to much. I turn his words over in my head, wondering where he ever got such a crazy notion. Not only do I have a personal history that informs me that want is more tenuous than need, but I have a cultural view of the world that says that the worth of women and girls is calculated based on what we can provide for others.

I really want to believe him. I want to feel like things are going to be okay. Maybe my lens is skewed and bent from years of trauma, and his carefree childhood taught him something else entirely. I decide to try and live in his world for a while and see if it helps. If nothing else, I'm incredibly relieved that he doesn't hate me and want to send me away.

It takes almost as much courage for me to tell Mom I am being treated for depression as it did to admit to Sean how I was feeling. I don't tell her everything, and I'm not proud of the reason I tell her. It isn't because I think I'll get some emotional support or because I need her to mother me. I'm telling her because I want her to know that whatever plagued her when I was little has somehow found its way to me. I want her to know that even though she seems to have worked her way through it, it hasn't left; it simply jumped humans. I want to blame her for my depression. I want her to feel responsible for it, to feel bad, to acknowledge that my flaws are her fault.

Family Traits

n order to get my undergraduate biology degree, I had to take a plant systematics class. We studied plant anatomy and compared different types of leaves and seed shapes and learned about plant families. I didn't like the professor and found most of the material boring as hell, but I will never forget the day I learned that the delicately scented, pastel flowers of the sweet peas I love are a close cousin to the ugly, allergy-inducing yellow flowers of Scotch broom. This weedy-looking shrub that grows wild in every highway median in the Pacific Northwest, that causes my eyes to swell and itch and my nose to run, is related intimately to the pink and purple blossoms of sweet peas that I love to bury my face in.

Once I recognized the shape of the flowers with their fan-like top above a pinched blossom on both plants, I couldn't unsee it. Every time I walked through town and saw sweet peas winding their way up and through my neighbors' chain-link fences, sporting their Easter-inspired blossoms, I cringed and held my breath.

Then I learned that the seeds of the regular pea plant, which I remembered shelling in the hot sun with my cousins and aunt in the mountains high above Santa Barbara, were delicious and sweet, while the seeds of the sweet pea would send me to the hospital in convulsions were I to pop one in my mouth.

Sitting in the stuffy lab, peering through a microscope with an X-Acto knife in one hand and a pick in the other, I loved the slow dawning of recognition that came over me as I dissected specimens. The clear hierarchy of the dichotomous key at my side revealed patterns that helped me make some sense of the world. I was able to put even wild things into some semblance of order, moving trait by trait, asking yes or no questions, going where the answers led me. Leaves or needles? Leaves, go to 2. Simple or compound leaves? Simple, go to 5. Leaves opposite each other or alternate on stem? Alternate, go to 6. In a few, clear steps, I arrived at the incontrovertible answer. And if I was wrong, I just had to retrace my steps and figure out how to do it right.

I felt the same satisfaction in math class when a particular concept allowed me to solve the most intractable problem in a distinct, repeatable way. I loved my Cell Physiology teacher more than I could express the day I discovered that the concepts I worked so hard to master in Organic Chemistry perfectly explained the mechanics of the Krebs cycle. I nearly hugged her. There was a method to the chaos. I just had to find the pattern!

When Mom's dad died, I offered to help two of my aunts and my uncle clean out his condo. Together, we discovered a closet full of cheap products designed to solve problems that only existed on late-night TV—things with names like ShamWow and Lazer Bond and Furniture Feet. Most of the packages were stacked, unopened, and we laughed as we called out their names to each other in TV announcer voices.

Deeper in that same closet, we came upon a box of photos, sepia-toned and faded, some sporting Grandpa's distinct, spidery handwriting on the back. Most of the others were a mystery. There were tiny 3-x-3 snapshots and a few 8 x 10s, lots of candid shots featuring round-faced children. I held my breath as I lifted each brittle photo carefully from the box and summoned the others to help me figure out who these people were. There were a few that my aunts and uncle recognized—a formal portrait of my grandparents on their wedding day, a shot of my grandfather with his brothers as a teenager—but the majority were photos of people none of us could identify.

There was a remarkable family resemblance in nearly every shot, though—I saw the round face of my aunts and my mother and my grandfather's long, graceful tapering fingers echoed in photo after photo. For generations, I saw the smile that turns to crow's-feet because everyone in this clan smiles with their whole face. I saw the freckles that dot our arms so heavily that they eventually run together to form Rorschach blots throughout these pictures. Sitting there, I felt a history, a connection, a kinship.

But I also felt fear. Are there some things we can't escape? Are there behaviors or mental processes that exist like dark spots on our DNA just like the freckles on my arm? My mom and her sisters all laughed the same way, gestured the same, sat the same. Was there some eternal cycle that made its way down to me no matter how hard I tried to be different? In my most fearful moments, I sometimes reach back in my mind for that dichotomous key, ever hopeful that it will go beyond showing me the order of things and instead, offer some sort of road map to ultimate predictability. In my most cynical moments, I place the blame for my flaws squarely on my mother.

Mom is curling her hair in the guest bathroom, and I sit on the end of the bed and watch her. She can see me in the mirror but this way, I don't have to look her in the eye. Her hair has continued to thin, and she's put on a little weight, but it keeps the skin of her face from being too wrinkly. We have the same nose, but otherwise we don't really look alike. The corners of her mouth rest in a frown and mine don't—at least not yet—and I hope they won't ever. She wears the same makeup she has for the last twenty years—orangey foundation that stops in an abrupt line at the edge of her jaw and her hairline, Maybelline black mascara that clumps a bit at the ends of her lashes, and grey-blue eye shadow. I've stopped wearing any makeup at all because I'd rather get an extra ten minutes of sleep in the morning than apply something I'll just end up having to take off at the end of the day. She is partial to elastic-waistband denim pants with huge pockets for her tissues and gum and the ever-present stack of business cards, and she always wears a blazer or jacket. We both love shoes and jackets and have way too many, but the similarities between us are few. I am much more like my dad. She was right about that.

Because we aren't looking each other in the eye, I gather the courage to tell her I am struggling with anxiety and depression. So that she doesn't think I'm asking for her help or advice, I add that I am on medication and going to therapy and working on holding it together.

"You know, Kari, after your dad left, there was a day when I called a babysitter to come stay with you guys. I got in the car and drove to the lake and parked right up at the outlook. I cried and cried and sat there trying to decide whether to take the car out of Park and just drive over the edge."

I go cold. For a millisecond, I feel what I think must be compassion, but then I force myself to remember all the times she locked herself away in her room, the fact that she sent us away to Wyoming, the times she let me take over and be Katy's mom without acknowledging how hard it was, that I was eight years old, that I had lost just as much as she had. Any compassion I felt immediately went up in flames, replaced with anger and resentment.

"What made you decide not to?" She still hasn't turned around to face me, and I'm rooted to the edge of the bed. This conversation could go sideways in a hurry if we don't tread lightly.

"You kids."

I nearly choke.

"After I drove home, I called my pastor. I told him everything and he started counseling me, helping me understand that everything is part of God's plan..."

I tune her out. This isn't God's plan. This is a cycle. A legacy of depression that I am not passing on to my daughters. I am more determined than ever to be different than she was, to be a better mother, to actively combat the urge to disappear, to check out. I will show them a different way. But I also know that perfection is not something I can strive for any longer, because it will destroy me.

I nod my head, stand up, and leave the room to check on the girls.

Heart Openers

In therapy, I begin a journey toward good enough. As I describe my daily life, the lessons I work to impart to the girls, the life I provide for them, the people I hope they become, my therapist's face changes. Her energy shifts from calm acceptance to skepticism as she cocks her head, leans forward, and pulls her eyebrows toward each other.

I stop talking midsentence and challenge her. "What?"

"You are trying so hard to be Supermom. Good, healthy, hot, nutritious meals three times a day. Mental stimulation, emotional support for the girls and Sean. A tidy house, always on time for things, play dates to enhance the girls' social skills, doctor and dentist appointments on schedule. Seeing that everyone gets enough sleep and not too much TV and some physical exercise every day, right?"

None of this sounds bad to me. I'm confused.

"What do you want?" she asks me.

"That. That's what I want."

"No, it isn't. Or you wouldn't be here. You are miserable. And what's more, you're setting your daughters up to be miserable."

That gets my attention.

"Where is the flexibility for mistakes or spills? How do they learn if they don't get those? And what about spontaneous resting time or boredom? Does that ever happen?"

"There will be time for that. They learn at school. And I'll rest when Sean isn't traveling so much, when they're older. They need me right now."

"They need you to be human, Kari. Listen, do you realize that your daughters are learning as much from watching you as they are from hearing what you say to them? They see that you put all of your efforts into making everyone else's life perfect and smooth. They see that you have no needs of your own, or that your needs don't matter. *And that's what they think mothers do. Who mothers are.* They see you utterly exhausted to the point of tears most days, and they are internalizing the message that they will be expected to be Supermoms one day, too. Is that what you want them to believe?"

No. It isn't. Decidedly not. Fuck. I still haven't figured out how to properly take care of anyone.

In an effort to figure out what it is that I want, I start writing. It's something I can do in small spaces of time, when the girls are at school or sitting in the lobby at the gymnastics facility while they're in class. At first, the thoughts come so quickly it's hard for my hand to keep up with the words pouring out of me, and the pages are generally filled with many more questions than answers. But over time, I begin to marvel at how powerful it feels to see my thoughts in print, and how something that forms in my brain can come out looking so different on paper.

I begin to recall that, while I was drawn to science and math in school because of their concrete, Right and Wrong nature, I also spent much of my youth with my nose in a book and I wrote some truly awful, tortured poetry in high school. There is something cleansing about putting my thoughts and feelings down on paper, and I start writing a blog, thinking that maybe preserving some of this for Erin and Lauren to look over one day might help them understand me a little bit more.

Mom calls and she's crying and talking so softly, I have to step outside to hear her. The girls are having a dance party with the dog in the playroom, and there's no way I can understand what she's saying.

"Ken has to go in for major heart surgery. Kari, I'm so scared."

Mom's husband Ken quit smoking after forty years when they got married, but the cumulative damage of those years has caught up to him.

"What are they doing?" I switch to medical assistant mode and explain what a quadruple bypass entails and how it will help. She wants to know how long he'll be in the hospital. The two of them are joined at the hip. Mom never was very good at being alone.

An idea blooms in my head. What if I go down for a few days and help out? I can lay in a supply of healthy meals for them to eat when he gets home, walk the dog and feed the cats, and let her just hang out at the hospital with him as much as she wants to. The girls are old enough to be just fine here with Sean, and I can use the time at her place to snoop.

Off and on throughout the years, I have searched for Cameron, but even with the Internet, it's a challenge because I don't know his real birth date or his real name or exactly when he was taken from us. Asking Dad and Mom is no use. Dad says he can't remember. He's sorry, but it was a tumultuous time and he left all the paperwork with Mom.

I have bugged Mom over and over again, my heart racing to work up the courage to bring it up when we talk on the phone, but her two stock responses involve refusing to talk about it and hanging up on me. I take advantage of her weakened emotional state to ask one more time.

"I'm not going to give up, Mom, and I'm not going to use the information for some awful purpose. I probably won't even contact him because I don't want to stir up his life if he is happy now. I just need to know, for my own sanity, that he found a family that loved him and cared for him and he is okay."

She screams through the phone. "They took him away from me on MOTHER'S DAY! It was the worst day of my life, and I've never been able to enjoy Mother's Day since then."

I am dumbstruck. None of that is true. She has never seemed morose or nostalgic on Mother's Day—never once uttered his name.

"Mom, it was a school day," I say quietly. "I know it was. I remember coming home through the alley and watching the van drive away with him in it."

"No, it wasn't. It was Mother's Day. And nobody told me. I had no idea. It was a total surprise. They just showed up to take him away and I never could stand Mother's Day again. What a cruel joke!"

I am stunned into silence. There are so many holes in this story. It makes no sense at all. Who comes on Sunday to undo an adoption? And who comes on Mother's Day? How could she possibly believe any of what she just said?

"I take it back. Your father knew. He must have. Cameron's suitcase was packed." Her voice drips hatred.

I can't go down this road with her. Even after twenty years, she still hates Dad more than anyone else. I have to change my approach.

"Do you have the adoption papers? Can I see them? I won't do anything without telling you first. I just want to see them. There are so many things I can't remember."

"No. Nothing. I don't think there were any papers. They told me later that the reason they took him away was because your father refused to sign the final adoption papers twice. They would rather have Cameron in a home where he was wanted."

There is a familiar sick feeling in my gut. I'm getting nowhere. I am Chicken Little.

The sky is falling!

The sky is falling!

My reality is met with disdain and denial. Am I crazy? I feel eight years old again, weighing my desire for family and belonging against the strong sense that everyone else is completely mistaken about what is happening. When I was eight, I chose belonging. I chose their Real, because my need to be part of that family was more important than anything else. I developed tunnel vision, like a mouse baited with cheese. I followed that trail and ignored the bigger picture around me because it meant survival.

When I try to force myself to remember details of things, put together complete pictures of events that feel incontrovertible to me, I either find empty space or come up with disparate fragments of things.

Philodendrons in macramé hangers

Karen Carpenter on the radio

Matching Dorothy Hamill hairdos for me and my mother

That time when I begged my parents to let me change my name to Debbie

As they form in my head, I am stunned. These things feel like details I ought to have remembered before now. They seem like things that should have made up the entire backdrop of my childhood.

Yellow-stained drinking glasses with mushrooms painted on them

The carpet in my brothers' room that had the perfect tile-like squares for us to use as city blocks when we played with Hot Wheels

I know there are more—things that were part of the landscape of any typical childhood that disappeared when my sister and I were molested—but there are black holes that no amount of therapy seems to be able to bring back. I don't remember the name of my fourth-grade teacher. I have ribbons and medals from track meets I don't recall running. I don't remember practicing piano or how old I was when I stopped taking baths and started showering. I don't remember learning how to sew, but I remember Mom's sunny sewing room with the old machine that folded down into a desk for storage, and somehow I remember knowing how to sew well enough by the time I was in high school that I made my own dress for the Junior Prom.

When my child mind blocked the things Clayton did to us, it shrouded so much more than that. When the memory of the abuse came back, almost two decades later, other things—mundane, pleasant things—stayed hidden.

Sometimes I wish I understood how memory works, so that I could peel away the black cover and find those other things, glittering like fool's gold in the stream of my mind. But other times, I wonder if I really want to know. Maybe I should be careful what I wish for. After all, those were the same years when my parents got divorced and I don't ever remember exactly what they fought about. Maybe that's why. Maybe there is more that my eight-year-old self thinks I should stay away from for my own good.

Mom has always been one of the most articulate people I knew, even if she didn't always tell the Truth. She is a wordsmith, and she knows just how to tell a story that fits her longing for a certain sequence of events. Over time, she tells the same stories so many times that they become real to her, even if I know things couldn't possibly have happened that way.

"Mom, that's not true. Don't you remember . . .?" I used to whine as her eyes flashed with anger. She flapped her hand at me as though my words were pesky houseflies, and if I persisted, she turned on her heel and stormed out. Her heels were always dry and cracked and when she pivoted, the rough edges caught on the carpet like Velcro and made a ripping sound as she steamed away from me.

I used to long for the day when I was a grown-up. When I would have enough agency to challenge her and be believed. Nobody believes kids. Every grown-up I knew was convinced we were all little liars.

"Fabricator," my dad used to accuse, as if using a bigger word sounded more serious. It did. I felt like I was on the witness stand in an episode of *Perry Mason*.

Perry Mason

M*A*S*H

The Bob Newhart Show

How do I know about those shows?

For years, I've told people that we didn't have a TV growing up. I don't remember watching television as a kid. I don't ever remember sitting down in the basement on the couch with my brothers and sister, staring at the television. In college, my friends played a drinking game that involved '70s TV show theme songs, and I always lost. I didn't know any of them. Occasionally, a song tingled at the edges of my mind.

The Flintstones

Hawaii Five-O

The Love Boat

How do I know what these theme songs sound like? I swear I didn't start watching television until long after my parents divorced, and I visited Dad and Susan.

Dad loved television. When I was in high school, and I visited one weekend a month, we sat in front of the TV at night, enormous bowls of vanilla ice cream varnished with Hershey's chocolate sauce in our laps, and watched Hawkeye Pierce and the crew save lives in Korea. Dad laughed so hard he got tears in his eyes. He roared back and slapped his freckled knee and looked at me to see if I thought it was just as funny as he did. I loved watching him laugh like that, but I never understood why *M*A*S*H* was Dad's favorite show. He never spoke of his time in Vietnam and if anyone asked about it, his eyes hooded over and his hands shook.

Even then, I knew kids weren't to be trusted. Maybe especially then.

High school kids are master manipulators, only interested in what they can get away with and how to make adults feel sorry for them. I lied to my parents all the time. I lied to my sister and told her everything was going to be okay. I lied to my teachers and told them I was fine. But in my mind, those were lies about little things. They weren't outright denials of the facts of my life; they didn't twist history. I needed more information about my history. There were too many holes. Too many memories gone, displaced.

It seemed like I was never old enough to challenge Mom's version of events. And then, when I was, I had to choose between having a relationship with her and being Right.

Once I was an adult, her response to my questions changed. Instead of dismissing me and getting angry, she cocked her head in confusion and questioned me with her eyes, a little line appearing vertically between her eyebrows. I was never quite sure if she was trying to jog her own memory to see if she maybe had gotten it wrong, or if she was trying to figure out how I could be so ignorant. In any case, she never changed her basic premise that our childhood was idyllic and perfect, until Dad ruined it and forced a divorce. That, had Dad just not cheated on her, we would have had the quintessential happy suburban family experience and lived happily ever after. She might have altered the stories from time to time, but they almost never aligned with my experience. Fortunately for her, the holes in my memory made me a lot less convinced of my position when I tried to flesh out the details, but my intuition and the sensate perceptions I had didn't scream "idyllic."

Mom came up to stay for a few days one time when Sean was on a business trip. She and the girls sat at the kitchen table, coloring, and I overheard Mom claim that she never spanked us. She told Erin and Lauren that she loved us too much to ever do such a thing. She said that only my dad—their Papa and Mom's bitter enemy—ever did anything so awful.

My mouth went dry as I stood at the sink, rinsing the maple syrup off of the plates before stacking them carefully in the dishwasher. I barked a laugh, and all three heads turned.

"You broke a wooden spoon over Chris's butt, Mom. How can you say something like that? You spanked him so hard with that spoon that it broke in half." As soon as the words left my mouth, I knew I shouldn't have said them. I was probably scaring the girls. Now they would worry that if Gram got upset with them, she might smack them with something snatched out of the yellow crock on the counter. The idea of someone they loved hitting them was terrifying. Their eyes grew wide.

"That may well have been the last time you ever spanked one of us," I continued in a softer voice. "You were as shocked as the rest of us, and I don't remember a wooden spoon ever coming out after that."

Mom's face didn't even get red. It just stayed blank as she looked at me. She wasn't defensive or angry or embarrassed. She just stared at me steadily and calmly.

"I don't remember that at all. I don't remember ever spanking any of you. And I certainly don't remember breaking a wooden spoon over anyone's bottom." She picked up her crayon and turned back to the picture of Cinderella.

———

Years after I remembered being molested by Clayton, I began to have flashes of mundane memories—exploring the empty lot behind our house in Klamath Falls, the Holly Hobbie bedspread I loved so much, piano lessons at my friend Jacque's house once a week. The memories came at odd times and yet there were still impenetrable lapses. I couldn't make them show up, and I couldn't figure out how to trigger them. I tried in therapy. I tried talking to my brother and sister. I asked Dad. He laughed at me.

"I don't remember everything from my childhood, either, Kari. That's normal."

Was it? I became fascinated with memoirs—especially childhood memoirs. I read about Bonne Bell Lipsmackers and thought *holy cow, I remember those!* I marveled at the ability of other people to conjure up details of birthday parties in grade school. *Did I go to any? I don't remember any birthday parties. I don't even remember any of my own birthday parties. Not one.* Years later, I've seen photographic evidence of my childhood birthday parties, and I still don't remember them. It's as if someone photoshopped me in to some generic '70s scene.

I imagine that time like a whirlpool, indiscriminately dragging down items from my psyche in order to obliterate the horrible things I simply couldn't process. I don't remember being nine or ten. I don't remember being six or seven, either. There are a few things that have burped up over the years, but the vast majority of my memories were removed and replaced with blank, black space. I suppose it took all of my energy to simply survive, and the effort of staying safe simply sucked everything else down into nothingness. Once I was no longer vulnerable, I could begin to form new memories, but not before then. The weight of combined losses in such a short period of time simply subsumed everything else, extending its reach beyond the months in which they happened to months and years before and after, like volcanic ash traveling hundreds and thousands of miles beyond ground zero to settle atop cars and houses and streets, evidence of great trauma.

Is it possible to reverse a black hole? Can you find something with enough gravitational pull to draw out the things that were sucked in? I sometimes think that if I can just manage to remember every last detail of the losses, good memories will cling to them like shreds of meat on a bone. There had to be good days in there, days where I felt like a kid—happy and carefree and safe and loved. I think I'm strong enough to try and remember everything about my parents' divorce, the months before and after Cameron was taken away, the sounds and smells of Clayton's bedroom. Especially if I get some of the joyous moments back, too. Maybe I would remember what it felt like to stroke the soft fur on my cat Misty's ears and head. Maybe I would recall a special song I used to sing for my sister at bedtime or maybe that we held hands across the divide between our twin beds and talked into the night, made up stories, giggled together.

Or maybe it's an exercise in futility. Perhaps I will continue to get the occasional flash of insight here and there until Alzheimer's whisks all of it away. I suppose it's possible that my mind has known what it was doing all along—protecting me from the awful things and slipping some of the good memories back in here and there when I need them to add juice to the essays I'd begun to write or as an example of the joy I've had in my life.

But I refuse to give up. I am an adult, which means I can challenge Mom's view of the world if I want to. Even if I set aside what I think I know to be true, there has to be some paper trail somewhere. No adoption agency would have flown a kid halfway around the world and placed him with a family without sending a packet of photos, background information, forms to sign. At some point there was something and someone has it. I make plans to stay with Mom and Ken for four days.

I come home with only a scrap of paper with the name "Dot Oulong" written on it. My search was almost entirely foiled by Mom's insistence that we do everything together, but I did manage to find this piece of paper inside a folder containing Katy's adoption paperwork while Mom was helping Ken change his bandage the day I left.

Starting there, I type "Holt Adoption Services," "Filipino," "Dot Oulong," and "Eugene, Oregon" into the search engine and follow a link to the adoption agency website.

Photos of smiling children form collages, tempting would-be families to choose them. I can't breathe. My stomach twitches, and my mouth fills with hot saliva. I slap the computer closed and curl up on the floor. The dog shuffles over to lick the tears off my cheeks, and we stay like that for a while.

The next day I try again, get a phone number, and call when the girls are at school. The woman on the other end tells me she's sorry, but without a birth date or the specific name of the orphanage or a social security number, she doesn't even know where to look for the files. They're all stored off-site in some warehouse somewhere, and it would take weeks to find records on one child even with that information.

My therapist suggests yoga. I have a couple friends who go regularly, and they invite me to join them twice a week when the girls are in school. After a month, I start to feel physically stronger and while I feel guilty that it's not cardio, I get the same euphoric feeling after yoga class that I used to get when I ran.

I've been going long enough that I know many of the instructors, and I can sense when they are going to change things up a bit. This morning, Mary is all about what she calls "heart openers." I set up my mat in the middle of the studio, and I'm looking forward to learning some new positions. Warming up, we go through the standard set of sun salutations a few times and then she asks us to prepare for camel pose. I've never done it, but I've seen it, and it doesn't look as hard as the arm balances I can never manage to accomplish. I move my knees to the top of my yoga mat, shins and the tops of my feet flush against the floor. Knees bent, I face the front of the room, and Mary asks us to sit up straight and tall. So far, I'm good.

"Rise up through the crown of your head and expand your lungs, shining the beacon of your heart to the front of the room. Now, pull your shoulder blades down and together, letting your chest rise up even more. Gradually begin to reach your hands back to the small of your back and arch into it. If you can, reach your hands to your heels and rest them there, shining your heart up to the ceiling."

I hold my palms to the small of my back and start to panic. My esophagus slams shut and I can't breathe. I have to fling myself forward into a neutral position in order to shake it off and inhale deeply. Whoa. What is this? I try again and the same thing happens. My heart races, my face flushes, and I have to pull up again and again or risk having a full-blown anxiety attack right here in front of the whole class. Emotion catches in my throat, and I slide into child's pose and cry quietly until it's time to move on to the next set of poses.

As soon as I get home, I open my laptop and look for information on camel pose. One website explains that most people get an endorphin rush in this pose, and that it helps with lymph drainage, massages the internal organs, and strengthens the spine. It is fairly typical to have an emotional response when attempting camel pose. One quote that stands out reads that "camel pose represents the ability to accomplish the impossible and go through life's challenges with ease. If you feel disconnected from the world, family/relationships, or are struggling with forgiveness, practicing camel pose can help you express yourself and find compassion for others."

I sit and think about the poses I enjoy and can do with ease, the ones that make me feel strong and accomplished—happy baby, pigeon, warrior 4. Hip openers. I feel a little disgusted that, as someone who was molested, I prefer a hip-opening pose to a heart-opening pose.

The next time I head in to the yoga studio, my excuse for not doing camel rests on my lips, but it turns out I don't have to use it. Today, Mary doesn't include it, but she does ask us to get in to full pigeon and as I relax in to this asana, imagining the tendons and muscles of my hips releasing with each breath, I revel in it.

At home, I close the door to my bedroom and unroll my mat. I position my knees at the top of the mat and ground myself mentally and physically. I close my eyes and begin to arch my back and reach my hands behind me for my heels. Bile rises in my throat, and I begin to hyperventilate as tears build just above the notch in my throat. I rest there and let them fall unchecked until I collapse to the floor in a heap.

Managing

I f there is unexpected blood, hysterical shrieking, a sudden disintegration of one's life or relationships, my focus sharpens. I shut out all of the other noise and channel my energy to the part of my body or brain most necessary to get you the hell out of there and back onto solid ground. I am great in a crisis.

These skills were important in the operating room, and as a mother. They are also often relied upon in my new role as front office person at the girls' Montessori school. This job doesn't pay well or draw on my college education or have the potential to advance my career, but it follows the same schedule as the girls and it allows me to get out of the house and my own head and spend time with adults. And at least once a day, I hold a tissue to a bloody nose, or bandage a cut, or break up a fight, or clean up little kid barf, which makes me feel useful in some tangible way. I am competent and kind and taking care of someone who can't take care of themselves.

But the day Dad calls me to tell me he has been diagnosed with lung cancer, I know those skills won't help at all. Witnessing ongoing pain is not something I do well. I have a strong desire to fix the broken, stop the bleeding. The single biggest challenge I've faced as a mother is allowing my girls to feel the pain that won't kill them. My instincts tell me to take it on for them or work to alleviate it as quickly as possible, both because I hate knowing they are hurting and because I hate witnessing it. I am learning how to sit with it, though, because the alternative is to pretend that it doesn't exist or shrug my shoulders and say, "it's not that bad," and I already know that approach is a recipe for disaster. Dad's cancer will be the biggest test of my ability to witness pain thus far.

I feel as though I am being carved away, piece by piece. Wave after wave of grinding agony peels layers of protection away as I watch Dad suffer. His skin is grey against the sterile white sheets. Two thick yellow tubes emerge from his back and bubble into a metered box partially hidden below the hospital bed. He shifts from his back onto his side, pushing against the mattress for leverage to relieve the pressure from the incision. A row of twenty or so staples winds its way down his shoulder blade and disappears beneath his left arm. His grimace is permanent at this point, but it deepens from time to time. His full head of hair is a disadvantage now, reflecting how long it has been since he has had a shower or a comb to tame it.

The heaviness in my chest feels like a sandbag, but instead of protecting me, it pulls deeper and deeper into me with each passing minute. I feel a crater threatening. Watching my larger-than-life father lie defeated and in pain, I long for some clear purpose or way to make this better. I hold his hand and we talk softly and watch TV. I tell him that I'll take the dogs for a walk and feed the birds and make sure the pantry and fridge are fully stocked. His wife is out with her parents right now, taking a break from the emotion of watching this fiercely independent man brought to his knees.

Dad is released from the hospital on Sunday and returns home half a lung and several lymph nodes lighter. The pallor of his skin is replaced by an unmistakable joy at being in his nest again, surrounded by pets and family photos with a view of his meticulously cared-for backyard. Katy comes for a visit and stays for dinner and Chris comes by to watch baseball and "shoot the shit." These are precious gifts. I feel whole when they are here, this is my family. My efforts to ease Dad's transition home are helpful, and I am so pleased. The quiet calm and purposeful activity are a powerful balm, and the grinding pain of the past week has opened up a new space inside me that is filling with love and gratitude.

He is optimistic that he will recover. A fit, athletic sixty-three-year-old who never smoked and rarely drank and played racquetball and squash every week—there is no reason this should be a death sentence. We make plans to have the girls come visit him when he is more mobile, and at the end of the week, I leave for the long drive home feeling exhausted but peaceful. I am at my best when I am taking care of people I love.

Dad calls me every week to share insights. He knows I am seeing a therapist, and he decides that it might be helpful for him, too. I am shocked and incredibly pleased. I never imagined that he would do something like this, but it seems to be having a big impact. He expresses remorse for some of the choices he made when we were kids, and I am unsure whether to let him talk or stop him and say it doesn't matter anymore.

He is scared. He says he doesn't want his wife to know, and he is determined to fight the cancer with everything he's got, but he is afraid, and I can't help but feel overwhelmingly honored that he is talking to me about it. I buy two copies of Pema Chödrön's book *The Places That Scare You*, and send him one so we can read it together. I'm not sure if he will or not, but it's worth a shot.

I remember the letter I wrote to Dad several years ago after reading Tracy Kidder's book *My Detachment*. I had, of course, learned about the Vietnam War in school, but I had never read a first-person account of what it was like, and it was jarring to think about my father as a young man, a young husband, being sent half a world away from everything he knew. I tried to imagine what it might have been like to see young men all around him dying, to write letters to their families, to write letters to Mom. Although he had never talked about Vietnam with any of us, and had no ties to anyone he had served with that I ever saw, I was certain that those memories weighed heavily on him, and that holding them so tightly must have been an enormous burden. I wrote that I understood why he may not want to revisit those memories and I didn't want him to talk about them if it was too painful, but I hoped he knew how badly I felt for the kid he was—newly married, newly graduated from college with his whole life ahead of him—suddenly yanked a world away to a jungle where his job was to kill other young men. Where his life was not his own, but was dependent on being in the right place at the right time, with land mines exploding around him and his team members dying right in front of him, not knowing if he would ever get the chance to meet the child his wife carried in her belly. I told him I loved him and that while I couldn't ever fully understand, I had a deeper appreciation for what he must carry every day.

He didn't write back, but he did acknowledge the letter. He thanked me and said it was too painful to talk about.

This time it's different. For more than a year, we read our copies of the book and have long phone conversations and exchange emails as we think about what is in it. This father-daughter book club is one of the most profound experiences I've ever had, and despite the reason for doing it, I feel more grounded and part of something than I can ever remember feeling. It is a powerful antidote to what I feel much of the rest of the time, which is helpless and sad.

————

I am sitting at the front desk at work when I notice my cell phone ringing. It's Dad. I grab it and step away to the laundry room where there are piles of towels and a basket of soiled little-kid underwear. I answer the phone and lean heavily on the washing machine, grateful that it isn't running at the moment because Dad is speaking so softly.

"Hey, kiddo. I'm sorry to call you at work but I just needed to ask you something." His voice is husky and low.

I am afraid.

"Okay, shoot. What's up?"

"So, I had an MRI last week because my legs have been bugging me— really sore. And they found some tumors in my bones. I'm thinking about radiation, but they took me up to the research hospital in Portland to do another scan first to see what my options are and there are some spots in my brain, too." His voice breaks, and he goes silent.

I wait.

"So, anyway, I want to know what you know about this new laser pen thing they can do for brain tumors. Does it work? Can I do it at the same time as the radiation for my legs? Is it safe?"

I clear my throat. "Well, what did the doctors say? Did you ask them this?"

"It's all experimental stuff and I can afford it, I guess, but Judy really wants me to go to Mexico for this other holistic treatment that she's been researching, and that's expensive, too."

They have been pulling out all the stops for the last six months—using both traditional chemotherapy and juicing and taking massive doses of vitamins and investigating alternative treatments like apricot seeds and acupuncture. I can't help but feel that if they're doing all of this, and the cancer has metastasized to his bones and brain in spite of it, there isn't much left to do.

"What does your gut tell you, Daddy? I can do some research and talk to some folks. I used to work in the radiology department up there, and I'm sure I have some contacts who are still there, but what does your gut say?"

It's so quiet for a few moments that I pull the phone away from my ear to make sure the connection isn't broken. Finally, I hear him breathe in sharply.

"I'm dying. It's over. Please don't tell anyone yet. You're the only one that can handle this right now."

I feel both proud and overwhelmed. I love that he trusts me with this assessment, and I hate being alone with it. I pull out a slip of paper I keep in my pocket with a quote from Pema Chödrön's book and read it out loud, for me as much as him:

> "Compassion practice is daring. It involves learning to relax and allow ourselves to move gently toward what scares us. The trick to doing this is to stay with emotional distress without tightening into aversion, to let fear soften us rather than harden into resistance.

"I'll stay here with you, Daddy. I promise. Even though I'm scared, I won't let it push me away. I love you."

All I can hear are sobs. I push a pile of underwear into the washing machine, drizzle some soap over the top of it, lower the lid, and push Start.

A month later, Dad is in hospice care, and I tell Sean we need to go to Oregon. We arrange for time off work, pull the girls out of school, and make the five-hour drive to Sean's parents' farm where we will stay. It is 20 minutes from Dad and Judy's house, so we can give them space, but I will be close enough to help.

I drive over every day to be with him, and I'm struck by how different he looks. He is completely bald from the cancer treatments, and his usually clean-shaven face is spotted with white whiskers. His once-muscular frame is gaunt and pale. He looks like I imagine he would at eighty-five, but he is only sixty-five. There is a tumor in his throat that protrudes out past his jaw and prevents him from talking or eating, and I sit with him as his sisters and father shuffle through quietly to visit, and neighbors bring casseroles and coffee and take Judy and the dogs to the park nearby. I hold his hand and drip morphine into his mouth to ease his pain and tell him stories of the girls that make him smile.

He squeezes my hand and looks at me with grateful eyes and when he sleeps, I pull out my copy of our book that has page after page dog-eared and marked up, searching for ways to cope with what I'm feeling.

When he is in physical pain, he gets agitated and tries to pull himself up on the rails of the bed. Sometimes I can see him trying to swing his legs over the side of the bed to get up, but his bones are so weak now that he could never stand. This restlessness, this desire to *move*, to do something to combat the physical pain, mirrors the emotional discomfort I'm feeling. I have an urge to peel my skin from my body, high-step in the middle of the room to release some of this energy, grind my teeth into dust. I hate this. I hate this. It is all I can do to stay present, reminding myself over and over again to breathe, to stop my wandering thoughts, to just sit with Daddy.

One morning a few days later, I am pouring myself a cup of coffee in my in-laws' kitchen, and my cell phone rings. It's Judy.

"Come now. It's almost time."

I drop my cup into the sink, find Sean on the sunny front porch to tell him I'm leaving, and ask him to get the girls dressed. I can barely hold his gaze. He knows. I shake my head and hop in the van as he hollers that they'll be right behind me.

I don't remember anything about the drive. When I walk in, the house is dark and silent. Judy sits in the family room, hunched over Dad's chest, and jumps up when she hears me come in.

"I can't do this anymore. I'm so glad you're here."

He is still alive, but he is struggling to breathe. They have tethered his arms to the bed so he can't push himself up, and his eyes are wild. I hug Judy and tell her I've got this. She leaves the room, and I search for the vial of morphine.

Leaning down close to Dad's ear, I whisper, "Hey, Poppy, it's Kari. I'm here. I'll make sure you're not hurting."

He nods and closes his eyes as I drip more morphine in to his mouth and within minutes he is asleep, breathing roughly.

Chris and Katy are on their way and Sean shows up with the girls, but they aren't sure they want to see him like this and I am not sure I want them to. Dad hangs on for a few hours as family members come through to say good-bye, and the hospice worker brings me another vial of morphine. I am giving him doses every 25 minutes now just to keep him comfortable, and I never leave his side. I am split in two. I am useful. I am bereft. I am helpful. I am scared. I am strong. I am destroyed.

A crowd stands in the sunny backyard, and at some point, I go out for a quick breath of fresh air. The family room is like a cave with the shades all pulled so the light won't bother Dad's eyes. As I stand near the koi pond he dug himself, watching the enormous fish swirl aimlessly, Judy pokes her head out the door.

"Kari!" she barks, and I run inside.

Dad's breath is crackly and frenzied. Judy sits on the couch near him, and I sit in the chair on the other side of his bed.

Leaning over him, I cradle his head in my arms and kiss him on the temple. I whisper, "It's okay, Daddy. You can go now. We're going to be okay. We will take care of each other. You don't have to fight anymore. You can let go. I love you."

He takes one last breath and dies in my arms.

———————

When I reflect on it a few days later, I realize that was the most beautiful and the most painful moment I have yet experienced. I am split in two, but not really. I am surprised to realize that when I am fully open to the feeling of anguish and the feeling of grace, the two can simply coexist without breaking me apart, even though it feels like they might.

In the months after Dad dies, I find myself overwhelmed from time to time. I talk to him a lot in my head, and I miss having him as a sounding board. There are days when I think I can't hold the painful emotions anymore, and it reminds me of the time I visited my grandfather in Santa Barbara right after they moved my grandmother to a long-term care facility because he could no longer care for her at home. She had early-onset Alzheimer's and he kept her at home as long as he could with a lot of help from my aunts and cousins, but at some point, he just couldn't do it anymore.

I hadn't seen Grandma or Grandpa in a few years, and I was shocked by my grandmother's decline. She was confused almost all the time and, in the months before they moved her, had wandered off more than once and been found miles away—one time at Payless with glass jugs of Gallo wine tucked under each arm. Grandpa had been reduced to a prison warden in his own home, watching his wife of over fifty years waste away physically and mentally, scratching all the grand retirement plans they had made together off the list of possibilities. This once-brilliant, personable, funny, athletic woman slept much of the time and was agitated and angry most of the remaining hours of the day. By the time I got there, Grandpa was bitter.

I had no idea what to say, but I couldn't just sit there and say nothing. I opened my mouth, and he cut me off.

"Don't you dare say what your mother said! That God never gives us more than we can handle. That is a load of bullshit! This *is* more than I can handle, and I don't for one minute believe any of that God stuff. I only went to church because it made your grandmother happy."

I was stunned. While I hadn't been about to spout that particular platitude, I'm sure whatever I had been about to say was equally as clichéd and useless. The only thing I could think to do was to put my hand on his freckled arm and squeeze as we let our tears spill.

I understand what he meant so much more deeply now. There are times when things happen that are more than we can handle. Maybe that's by design. Maybe the point is to acknowledge that we can't do it alone, so that we reach out for help. For most of my life, I thought asking for help was the definition of weakness. I saw my parents and teachers praising people who figured things out on their own, who were independent and capable. But the truth was, when I tried to handle everything by myself, all I felt was lonely and incompetent. While I may have eventually figured out how to tackle certain challenges, I'm positive it wasn't the most efficient way to go about it. It was also really bloody exhausting.

Human beings are social creatures who draw strength and information from each other. Even people who are held up as examples of pioneering spirit don't truly do it on their own—they build on the successes of those who came before them, or they benefit from the support and love of family and friends. Maybe being routinely faced with more than we can handle is the Universe's way of ensuring that we continue to find ways to work together and help each other.

I'm getting more comfortable with admitting when I'm overwhelmed or sad, and releasing the idea that it is somehow shameful to feel that way or to reach out. The truth is, my closest friendships have been forged through the process of asking for or being asked for help. The people I trust the most are those who recognized when I was in trouble and offered a hand without judgment, or who rose to the occasion when I cried out.

I am grateful for the gift Dad gave me by letting me support him and love him when he most needed it. The man who used to say that weakness was the worst trait a person could have, and that asking for help was a sign of weakness, turned out to be the one who helped me learn that it's actually a sign of strength. I think we learned that together.

Revelations

Thanks to the Internet, I can find our old house in Klamath Falls. I loved that house—the sunny yellow color with the white trim, the crabapple tree in the front yard with its craggy limbs and pink blooms in the spring. I spent hours pulling cherries out of the enormous tree in the backyard, splitting them open with my thumbs to see if there were any little white worms inside. Daddy built us a swing set of his own design with a sheet-metal slide that burned the skin off our legs in the hot Klamath Falls summers, and he installed a basketball hoop on the roof edge of the garage out by the alley for us to practice on.

It is amazing how certain memories of that house are so vivid, and yet I am shocked when I pull up an old real estate listing and see the particulars. Was it really only a little over 2000 square feet? Were there really only two bathrooms?

I am disappointed that there are no interior photos. I want to see if the walls are still painted yellow, if the kitchen still feels as sunny and bright as it does in my memory. The house was last sold in 1984—the year I finished junior high school. Whoever lives there has been there for a long time. I wonder if they raised a family there, if their kids enjoyed our swing set, if the basketball hoop is still there. I wonder if they know that a family moved there, fell apart, and left in bits and pieces, peeling off one at a time until Mom was the only one left.

I sometimes think about taking Erin and Lauren on a road trip to the places I grew up. I want to show them the crappy apartment with the silverfish in Forest Grove that I shared with their Uncle Chris, the big grey house with the view of the Pacific Ocean where I could watch the whales migrate in the spring when I came back from Wyoming. I think about driving south past Eugene and Grants Pass to Klamath Falls and pulling up outside that house on Del Moro Street with the steep slope that dead-ended at Kit Carson Park, so I can show the girls where my friend Jacque and I found kittens beneath a holly bush with their eyes barely open, and smuggled them home in our sweatshirts to convince our mothers to let us keep them. But I know that I can't go back to Klamath Falls now without walking across the street and through the alley to find the little white house with black trim where Jan and Clayton and Shauna and Stevie used to live. And I can't do that with Erin and Lauren because I'm afraid of what I might remember, standing in front of that house, walking through that alley, looking across the street to Roosevelt Elementary. As someone who finally feels somewhat competent as a mother, I worry about conjuring up that scared eight-year-old inside of me as I stand with my children, in case it breaks something open.

———

The day I find the box of Dad's letters, I can't do much beyond read them and brush the dog. Brushing the dog is never a satisfying task, given that forty-five minutes later, I still harvest as much hair as I did when I began. Even though he is nearly eighty pounds, I've made piles of dog hair big enough to hide him in after brushing him for ten minutes. But while it isn't satisfying, it is meditative. It allows for skittering thoughts, like rocks skipped across the surface of a lake. Sometimes I like to watch my thoughts to see how many times they touch down before they finally sink.

The letters were not something I expected to find. I was looking for boxes of DVDs that I had packed away a year ago, so that I could dust them off and put them back on the shelves in alphabetical order. I had hoped to discover a chick flick that was appropriate for Erin and Lauren so we could watch it together while Sean was out of town.

When I first open the box, I discover several smaller boxes with Dad's ancient slide carousels and I push them away to avoid the ache in my stomach. Two of them are labeled "Vietnam," and I remember spending one horrible afternoon clicking through the slides after Judy discovered them in his office closet. Nobody knew they even existed. Mom and Susan both said they'd never seen slides from Vietnam.

I sat and flipped through mostly benign images of Dad and his fellow Marines on the beach or playing cards in their camp, but eventually I came across a series of shots detailing a crew loading a helicopter with what I assume were canisters of Agent Orange. The men climbed into the chopper and Dad's camera followed it as it flew higher and higher into a beautiful blue sky in a series of slides. I noticed a speck in the left top corner getting closer and closer to the helicopter until, near the seventh or eighth picture, the speck and chopper met in an explosion. There was one more picture of fire in the sky and then nothing. No wonder Dad never answered my letter. He had literally photographed his friends and fellow Marines being shot out of the sky one impossibly gorgeous day in Vietnam.

I dig deeper and spot a manila folder with my loopy, adolescent cursive on the outside, "Kari Leigh." Lifting one side, I discover a full-color photo of Erin as a baby printed on plain paper. And then another, and another, and then her as a toddler and Lauren as an infant. Every photo of the girls I emailed Dad over the years had been printed out on a full sheet of paper. My dad, the most frugal person in our family, the guy who went around barking at everyone to "Turn the light out when you leave a room! Who do you think pays for this? Am I made of money?" had spent untold amounts of cash on laser printer toner—color toner—in order to preserve the candid shots of his granddaughters. I resist the urge to calculate what he must have spent. If he had asked me for reprints, I would have sent them to him.

Then come birthday cards and thank you cards the girls scribbled on for him. The Father's Day cards I chosen to be humorous but not biting, kind but not sappy. He saved every one.

The letters are in the bottom of the box. Dozens of letters and emails I sent to him over the years, dating all the way back to Klamath Falls and the divorce. He kept all of them—some addressed to him and Susan, others to just him, and still more sent to Dad and Judy. He even somehow had a copy of a note I wrote to Mom about how hard it was for me to say good-bye to him when he left to drive to Wyoming to start his new life. Some of my letters referenced letters he had written back to me. Suddenly, the urge to brush the dog hits me. I am agitated and restless. I have to do something with my hands.

It isn't the white-hot, breathtaking pain of his death that is so upsetting. This is the deep ache of regret. The letters I didn't save. The conversations we might have had. The things I never knew I might want to know later that I can't ask about now. Things like how he saw the civil rights movement in the 1950s and '60s, how much time he spent in Vietnam and how he felt about having to go, what it was like to come home. How he figured out what choices to make and how to live with himself after making mistakes and what his biggest dreams had been.

It is the things he won't be able to share with my kids like playing "Froggie Went a-Courtin'" on the banjo and teaching them to sing along. The times when he might have done something that prompted me to ask how he ever learned that or why he chose a certain path in life.

I want to know why he kept the letters. Did he ever sit in his office at home and read over them again and smile at my naiveté or wonder at my maturity? Did the letter where I wrote to him about his admission of regret—where I told him that I understand we are all human and I love him dearly and admire him a great deal—draw a tear or two? Did he reread certain portions or share them with his wife? Did he write back immediately or wait a while to compose just the right response? Who was my Dad, and how did he feel about being a father?

"Mommy? Come look at Eva, please," Lauren calls from upstairs.

I'm still unpacking the car from the road trip we took to visit Sean's parents, but she couldn't wait to dash upstairs and say hello to her hamster. I make my way to the bonus room, certain that Eva is just traumatized from having been cared for by the neighbors for the last four days, but when I get there, it's clear there is something wrong with her. It's late, and it's Sunday night, so our only option is the emergency vet, and Erin insists on coming, too, so the four of us pile back in the minivan and drive north in the dark.

Sitting in the exam room, Lauren moves from her chair to my lap to bury her face in my shoulder for a while. The vet has taken Eva to the back to assess her more fully, and the four of us are barely allowing ourselves to breathe as we wait. At one point, Lauren asks if I will take her back out to the dark waiting area with its cute photos of other furry patients and skeletons of exotic pets like snakes and chinchillas. I take her hand and lead her out to the deserted entry way, and she solemnly runs her finger over the bones of each skeleton and breathes deeply.

The vet tells us that she will have to keep Eva overnight, and Lauren nods her head and walks quietly to the car.

"Mommy, will Eva be lonely there by herself tonight?" Lauren asks me as I tuck her in to bed. "I feel so bad that we were away when she got sick. She must be scared."

I reassure her that Eva will be taken good care of and promise to call for a status update first thing in the morning.

Over the next two days, Eva gets progressively worse and I realize that I am going to have to have a "quality of life" discussion with Lauren. Sean has expressed astonishment at how much money we are spending on a $10 hamster, and I know it's time to let her go. I am not quite sure even how to have the conversation. I don't know what she remembers from Dad's death, but as soon as I sit her down to talk, she preempts me.

"Mom, if she is hurting, I don't want her to. If they can help Eva without hurting her and she can get better for a long time, let's do that. But if they are going to do surgery and she will hurt from it as she heals for weeks and then dies a few weeks later, that's not a good life."

I have no words. She has clearly been thinking about this for a while. We make the painful decision to let her go. After I get off the phone with the vet and let them know that we will be there later to collect her remains, Lauren climbs up into my lap again—filling it completely—and starts to cry.

"I am so confused. I don't know how to feel. I'm happy she doesn't hurt, but I'm sad she's gone. I'm happy I got to be her Mommy for a year and I know I was a good Mommy and I gave her a good life, but I don't want her to be gone." She isn't angry, and she doesn't rail at the unfairness of it all. She is simply allowing herself to grieve and hold all of the competing emotions at the same time inside her little body. She is my hero.

"I am so sorry you're sad, sweetheart. I wish I could do something to change it. As your Mommy, I often wish I could give you a life without sadness or pain. It hurts me to see you cry." I rub her back and nuzzle my face in her silky blonde hair. How can she sound so grown up and still smell like my baby?

"That's silly, Mom. I know that seems nice at first, but I wouldn't want a life that doesn't have upset or sad or angry feelings. That would be like having the sun shine all day long every day—no night, no rain, no snow. How boring would that be!"

I squeeze her tight and marvel at the wisdom she already possesses. How can I help her preserve this ability to simply feel what she is feeling and accept it?

A moment later, she climbs down and takes a deep, shuddering breath. She asks me if I will clean out Eva's cage and put it away because she thinks it will be too sad for her to do, and I jump at the suggestion, happy to do something tangible to help. Over the next few weeks, she comes to me a few times and asks to be held while she mourns for Eva. She passes by Erin's hamster's cage reverently and offers him treats, relishing her role of auntie without jealousy, and Erin offers to let her play with Tickle if she wants to. These girls are feeling their way through grief with grace and dignity, while I stand back and watch and learn.

Book Three:

The Halo

2012–present

By Heart

When I talk to Mom on the phone, I pay acute attention to her speech, vigilant for new lapses of memory. Lately, I've noticed she is dropping words, and I notice it again today when I call her. I begin every conversation talking about the weather because it's a safe topic. It doesn't require any sort of mental recall. It's doing what it's doing right now and all you have to do is look out the window and describe it. Sometimes, that leads to conversations about potential activities for today and/or what sounds good for dinner. If it's cold and stormy, soup sounds good, and from there, we can fantasize about different kinds of soup together.

Today, I am frustrated that it's raining because I hate walking the dog in the rain, but I'm heartened because it means we might have something to talk about. I whine a little about the rain squalls we have been having in Seattle for the past few days and ask Mom what it's like down in Salem.

"Well, there's no . . . There isn't any . . . water coming from the sky right now, but it's threatening."

I am struck by the fact that she can't remember the word "rain," but she still has the poetic ability to say something like "it's threatening." I'm also pretty impressed that she found a workaround by describing it—there's no mistaking what "water coming from the sky" means. Even after a long pause or two, she generally finds a way to express herself.

I imagine entire networks of neurons in her brain stopping short at one particular word that is obscured, backing up a little, scouting the area, and barreling off in a different direction that gets her to roughly the same destination. For some reason, I'm incredibly proud of her for finding these alternate routes.

But while I'm proud this time, there are other times when I have a sympathetic response not unlike what happens when a friend tells me their kid has lice, and I start to scratch my head. I know Alzheimer's isn't contagious, but it is genetic, so sometimes I freak out and wonder, *Have I started to slip? Is the fact that I can't keep track of Erin and Lauren's schedules in my head anymore a sign that I'm heading down the same path as her?* I begin to catalogue every instance in the last week when my feet have taken me to a room in the house that my brain can't recall wanting to go to or why.

They say that until you see something happen to someone else or experience it yourself, it remains almost unimaginable. You can walk the same stretch of sidewalk for years and never worry about being mugged, but after it happens once, every time you walk that same path, your body's physical response trumps any rational thought process you have and you start to freak out. It turns out, simply being in the same place where something scary happened triggers a cascading, automatic set of reactions that take a lot of effort to stop. Every time I forget something I thought I'd never forget, I think of Mom.

———

I didn't think that I could ever forget all of those parenting moments that other people take the time to meticulously record in baby books. As they were all happening—first haircut, first tooth lost in a trickle of pink, first pair of shoes—I was certain that every detail would remain lodged in my heart and mind, carbon copies for all time.

I know better now, and I wish I had done a better job marking those occasions. I think about the curious way Mom has lost certain memories and the way she denied other ones, and it makes me want to know how much influence my subconscious has over which things stick and which don't. Perhaps regular moments that are not imbued with emotion, threaded through with fear or anger or fierce love, simply glance off my brain like rocks skipped on the surface of a lake. But the memories encumbered by passion and sentiment sink into my psyche, imprinting themselves on the silty soil beneath and leaving a trail of pebbles for me to turn over and look at whenever I want to. The moments I recall most vividly are the ones whose airy pockets are stuffed with rank, sweaty fear, or a desperate desire to be anywhere other than where I was.

I recall Lauren's eyes, liquid with terror as violent stomach cramps nearly turned her inside out, thanks to a serious allergic reaction. She was certain she was going to die right there at Disneyland, vomiting over and over again into the bushes outside Pirates of the Caribbean. She was barely able to catch her breath as she heaved and I held her and screamed for Benadryl.

I will never forget the night six-year-old Erin held our cat while the veterinarian injected him with the poison that would put him to sleep. Her lower lip quivered and tears gathered in the corners of her eyes, but she was determined to be brave. I was simultaneously awed and heartbroken.

I haven't forgotten those moments where I wished for the power to obliterate their pain or, at the very least, encapsulate it and fill myself with it instead. Those are the moments I think I might never forget.

There are moments from my childhood that I am certain were pure emotion, that consisted almost entirely of a fogbank of fear or loathing, but it occurs to me that Mom may not have felt the same way, either because she didn't allow herself to or because of her perspective. If her mind works the same way mine does, then it makes sense that her adult self might not have seen things the way I did, and didn't imprint those things the same way.

But then there are the experiences that hid from me for decades and later surfaced for reasons I can't comprehend. Why did I remember Clayton molesting me so many years later, and why are there still so many holes? The things I have been able to remember are scattered and scrambled. Timelines cross and bend, and images appear like still photos in a slide show—moments that I see with a singular clarity but cannot fit into a particular place with any certainty.

I want to know what it smelled like inside Jan's house and what color my book bag was. I want to remember which pictures were on my lunch box and whether there was anything left rattling around inside at the end of the day. I want to know if I reacted to Clayton by crying or fighting or simply lay there waiting until he was done. I want to know why Katy never forgot and why my mind buried it.

Did those memories hurtle down toward the lake bottom of my mind with enormous speed, propelled by the sheer weight of emotion, and bury themselves so deeply that it took years to uncover them? Maybe that is why Mom can't remember so many of the things I want her to remember. Maybe, when she swears she only ever spanked one of us with a wooden spoon once and never again, she is speaking her Truth, and the rest of those spankings are buried deep in her mind. Maybe she has the same holes in her mind that I do, and her story about Cameron leaving was a desperate attempt to fill them in in a way that made sense and gave her some peace.

At some point, it occurs to me that one big difference between the things I can remember (Lauren puking in the bushes, Erin's despair at losing our cat) and the things I can't (Lauren's first day of kindergarten, Erin's first swim lesson) is fear. And, certainly, the things I can't remember that were trauma-filled were on some other level of fear altogether, so perhaps there is some tipping point, some sweet spot in the middle where memories are imprinted while others blow away with the wind or are buried so deeply they can't be retrieved.

––––––––

As the girls get older, I am grateful for social media, if only for the technological ability to record special moments. My computer contains row after row of "selfies" they have taken on the first day of school, of them walking on the beach during a family vacation, of the things they deem important and noteworthy. I suspect one day we will all look back in consternation, trying desperately to decipher why that particular moment felt vital to record, but it alleviates some of my guilt at not being able to catalogue all of the happy moments in my mind. Knowing that we will remember the saddest, scariest moments without photographic reminders, it is nice to have the digital balancing out of happy times tucked away in my laptop. If nothing else, their Instagram feeds are the reverse of the human brain: instead of emphasizing the negative in an effort to avoid danger, they portray the best moments, curated to present a happy, joyous life. As much as I hear this "false narrative" criticized by other parents, I am pleased to know that somehow, externally, the weight skews toward the positive when our brains are wired to do just the opposite.

Surrender

had lunch with Angel today. We have known each other since high school and just happen to both live in Seattle now. Even though our lives are very different—she is single and works with small local theatre groups, and I am married and a stay-at-home mother—we have a history that makes it easy to just be together and talk. She is letting me vent about being overwhelmed with kids and running the household while Sean travels as much as he does and then she starts to give me advice from a business class she took one time. I nearly fall over. Angel? Took a business class? She was a theatre arts major with a gorgeous singing voice. When did she take a class about business?

"Never mind that," she says, when I ask. Angel is a fast talker—someone my father would have called a motormouth—and she blithely refuses to be derailed. "Manageable chunks, Kar. Not prioritizing or triaging or placing importance on one set of tasks over another. Just manageable chunks."

It occurs to me that this is a vanilla enough phrase that it can mean just about anything to anyone. And that is precisely why I like it.

Today, editing my latest book review is not manageable. Neither is calling the naturopath's bookkeeper and the insurance company and the HSA administrator to fight about whether or not my deductible has been met even though it is December 12. Even less manageable is facing the number-crunching that has to be done for the landscaping project Sean and I are considering. You know what is manageable? Shopping.

And so, leaving the restaurant, I drive to some cute stores while the girls are at school to pick out stocking stuffers and purchase a book or two to round out my holiday gift lists. And then I decide that I can also handle coming home, hauling the wrapping paper and ribbons out of the attic, and staging a Santa's helper area for the girls to immerse themselves in.

Once I've picked them up from school and fed them a snack, we sit on the floor in the playroom swapping scissors for tape for ribbon and doing our best to make the packages look nice despite the black fur that sticks to everything (because the other thing that is not manageable is vacuuming), and I am pleased that I have given myself a break. Today, this is something on my to-do list that I feel I can tackle with the mindset, energy, and ability I have.

———

I am struck still when I see the news story about a lone, masked man who entered a busy shopping mall in Portland and began shooting randomly, killing two people and wounding a fifteen-year-old girl before killing himself. I know that mall. Katy used to work there. My friend Carrie took her son to visit Santa there just yesterday. I can't move. Can't breathe. Can't think.

When the shock leaves my body, I am at first sad and then grateful that more people weren't injured or killed. I wonder who this poor, angry man was and why this was the solution that came to his mind. And then I am still again because I have no answers.

Logically, I know I don't have all the answers. Viscerally, I disagree entirely. Logically, I don't even want to have all the answers. God forbid someone calls me up one day and say, "Kari? Good, you're there. I'm taking a break for a bit and I need you to mind the Universe until I come back, okay? Thanks."

I would wet myself. I would stutter and sputter and perhaps vomit. That is growth, because when I was eight or seventeen, I would have taken up the mantle with cocky assurance and complete conviction. I would have belligerently made my way to the throne and systematically set about fixing all that I believed was wrong with the world. In my twenties and thirties, I would have hidden and cowered or run away because I knew I had no answers at all.

But now, in my forties, I sometimes fantasize that whichever person *is* in charge will call and ask me for one piece of the puzzle. That I can eloquently and articulately present my argument for, say, organic food or single-payer health care or stricter gun control and leave them saying, "Damn! You're good! Of course, we will implement that right away. We are so glad we asked you. Can we keep your number in case we have other questions?"

The difference is one of scale, of wisdom, of equanimity. It occurs to me that every moment of every day there are things being done, things that I don't even know about or understand and didn't set in motion. And while they may not entirely cancel out or eradicate the things that make me gnash my teeth in anger or frustration, they constitute motion. Even as I notice a new crack in my index finger—a result of the eczema I deal with every year at this time—my body is working to repair some other damage or create some new cell somewhere else that I can't see. Maybe it is enough to give my finger a leg up by slathering some cream on it and trying to keep it out of hot water to allow my body's resources to be used elsewhere.

I am surely part of the solution, but only part. And I can only operate within the boundaries of what I know as Truth and do the rest of the Universe the enormous favor of not challenging every little thing it says or does. Because I don't have all the answers. And I can't see the whole picture, but I do know that everywhere, simultaneously, healing is happening at the same time as harm. And as long as I stick to my manageable chunks, progress is being made.

Ironically, admitting that I don't have all the answers is a bit freeing. While the Teacher's Pet in me kicks my shins furiously and sticks out her tongue, it is a huge relief to accept the fact that perhaps I don't have to go out and fix things all the time. And it is an even bigger revelation that part of the reason I have avoided certain people and situations in my life is because I felt as though I was expected to provide some solution that I honestly did not possess. While I generally chalked those avoidances up to less enlightened things like, "She's a total freaking mess and it's not my responsibility" or simply, "He's an ass," it turns out that what I was really avoiding was the fear of acknowledging the simple truth that I DON'T KNOW WHAT TO DO WITH THIS.

Once I face that fear and shove it out of the way, there is room for compassion—both for myself in all my ignorance and for that other person I wanted to blame or label, who is probably feeling really shitty or scared. Having spent most of my life trying to convince everyone that I was mature/intelligent/capable enough to handle anything, it's a little bit of a turnaround to suddenly realize I'm not. I suspect it will take practice and faith that somewhere, someone has a few of the answers I don't have. I have to trust that others have their own particular pieces of the puzzle. And me? I have my manageable chunks and my not-so-manageable chunks and I have a few answers, but I don't have them all.

Family Traits

"I'm still mad at you." Erin looks me straight in the eye without flinching. She doesn't raise her voice or emphasize one word more than any other. She is making a simple statement of fact. She is pissed off that I emailed her favorite teacher to check and see if she is okay. The dean of students told me when I came to pick Erin up today that she saw Erin crying in the hallway and thought it was noteworthy because she is incredibly stoic. I was alarmed, too, because Erin often proclaims that she only allows positive emotions in her life, so for her to cry publicly is unusual.

Because I know Erin will never talk to me about what's going on, I emailed the one teacher I know she adores. Even though I'm dying to know what happened, I resist the urge to ask for details, instead just asking Ms. D to reach out to Erin and support her.

I want to stop the car and defend myself when Erin says she's angry with me. I want to ask if she even read my response to her after Ms. D told her about my email and she texted me in all caps in the middle of math class:

I HATE YOU. THIS IS NONE OF YOUR BUSINESS. WHO TOLD YOU? STAY OUT OF IT!

I responded immediately with a text of my own:

I'm sorry. I love you. I wanted to make sure you had someone to talk to that you trust.

But right now, I decide not to respond. The remaining five seats in the car are full of Erin's basketball teammates, but it wouldn't matter even if they were empty. Erin has decided that the salient point here is that I didn't simply leave her alone. Instead of acknowledging her pain or my attempt to give her space, she wants to focus on figuring out who told me she was crying so she can go inform them that they had better not ever tell me anything ever again. I am not allowed to know anything about her life that she doesn't want me to.

I remember that contempt. That disdain. That certain knowledge that my mother could not possibly relate to me or my life or the reality that I trudged through each and every day. And that is the part that hurts—because I remember the scorn that burned in my belly for my mom and I wish I didn't. I hope she doesn't remember it.

It also sucks because I swore I'd be a better mother, that my kids would want to come to me with problems and triumphs. I'm beginning to realize it's not as simple as that. It doesn't really matter what I want and, in truth, so much of my desire to have her confide in me is to prove to myself that I'm doing this mothering thing right this time.

———

I once heard someone say that kids born in the 1970s are the least-parented generation. I don't know if that's even quantifiable, but I believe it. From making Shrinky Dinks and melting Barbie heads in our Easy-Bake Oven to Chris threatening to brand me with his wood-burning kit on more than one occasion, we were chronically unsupervised. I can still remember the exhilarating freedom of being sent out of the house right after breakfast on a summer morning and told to "stick together and be home before dark."

And yet, I hold so much resentment toward Mom for not being there, for not parenting, and it is such a double standard. I was angry with Daddy for cheating on Mom, for going off and making a new family, but I didn't have the same expectations of him that I did of Mom. I wanted her to be tender and loving and ever present. I wanted her to somehow read my mind and know what I needed.

Even as I got older, I still held on to some ideal of a mother-daughter relationship that she wasn't living up to. Not only was I angry that she didn't give me the childhood I thought I deserved, I was still angry when

I was planning our wedding and she couldn't remember much about her own wedding planning when she married Daddy. When my girls were born and I asked her what her experiences were like when we were first born, she didn't have much to say. I never asked Daddy any of those things. It would never have occurred to me to ask him.

Maybe some of her reluctance to dispense advice or commiserate was because, by the time I was an adult, I was already so resentful and angry that she knew it. Maybe she felt so burned by my rejection that she didn't want to risk being shoved away again. And, during the times when I really struggled as a mother myself and didn't call her, the excuse was that she wouldn't rise to the occasion, but the truth is, I never gave her the chance. At this point, I am painfully aware of what it takes to be both human and a mother, and I am more painfully aware that I never offered Mom the chance to be both at the same time.

I take the dog out for a walk in the clear, morning air. The leaves are just beginning to turn color and the sidewalks are littered with chestnut husks. We wander toward the elementary school just as class breaks for recess and as I hear joyful squeals rise, I think about how hard I have worked over the years to give my children the idyllic childhood I always wanted but didn't get. An old familiar resentment rises in my throat like heartburn, and I kick a rock in my path, sending it to the end of the block.

Much of my writing these days consists of letters to my daughters. I am desperate to have my intentions known. I note that I am working to respect their personal boundaries, that I am here to support them and not control them. I am effusive and loving and careful to remind them how proud they can be of themselves, calling out their strengths and straddling the line between flattery and gushing. And all the while, as my words come to the page, there is a wall of stone and mortar, on the other side of which lie my own teen years. As I write, my mind reaches out to brush fingertips along the rough surface of the stones and reassure myself that these two places, times, people, remain wholly distinct and separate.

I am not my mother.

My daughters are not me.

I will not abandon them.

I am a good mother.

I am beginning to realize that this wall is not a wall at all: it is a mirror that is showing me some version of my teenage self that I don't like. I do love my daughters, but I wonder how much of what I say to them is aimed at convincing myself that I was right and Mom was wrong.

The dog stops to pee, and a lump forms in my throat. How many years have I wasted being angry with Mom for not giving me the mother-daughter relationship I wanted? As she sinks deeper and deeper in to her own mind and her memories peel off a few at a time, I am left feeling ashamed. Assuming she understands what is happening to her, she is probably terrified. And the fact that I was angry about having to take care of her, sit with her in silence, or tell her the same things over and over again is incredibly petty. A wellspring of love and compassion bubbles up inside me. Maybe I can heal myself by smashing that wall and acknowledging that it was built of hurt and resentment and admitting that it never protected me from anything except having a relationship with Mom.

Of course, all of this is complicated by the feelings of responsibility I had for her for so many years. After that first time we visited her and Dallas when we lived in Wyoming, the tone of Mom's letters changed drastically, and instead of writing to all three of us together, she sent extra letters specifically for me.

She wrote that she hoped I liked Dallas and that we got home okay and all the regular stuff, but then it got weird. She wrote how much she loved and missed me and went on to say that she didn't think she could live without me. She begged me to ask Daddy to pay for us to come to the wedding and asked if I would think about moving to Lincoln City with them. It took me a while to write back because I hated talking to Daddy about money, and I felt so sad for her. I was trapped and confused. She had told us to stay in Wyoming, but now she wanted us back. Or just me? I didn't know.

Over the next few weeks I got more letters from her that said things like "I'm only half a person without you" and "You are my only purpose for living," and it made me feel like she wasn't giving up on me, that she really did want me around. I remember trying to convince Katy to move back to Oregon with me as soon as school was out because Mom's letters just kept getting sadder and sadder. I wondered if Dallas was getting sicker, and she was feeling alone again. She told me he said he was dying, but that she still wanted to marry him, and I felt like she needed me there so she wouldn't be alone with all of that. It was my first seductive experience with being needed by her and, as confusing as it was, it also made me feel like I was important. And it made me believe that I had some measure of control—that there was something I could do to make things better for someone else.

As my girls get older, I am learning that if you are a person who has made your children your life, it is hard not to lean on them when you need support. Also, if you are lucky enough to have mature, emotionally stable kids, when the rug gets pulled out from underneath you, it is powerfully tempting to ask them for help and support. And if both of those things are true—that your children are your life and they are mature and caring—it takes a great deal of courage and conviction to not divulge every little detail of your fear and despair, anger and disappointment and overwhelming sadness to them in the hopes that they will prop you up when you fall and remind you that they are on your side.

The closest buoy is the one we most often want to reach for, but if that buoy turns out to be my children, I know I have to keep on swimming. They need me to be a mother. It is not their job to be mine. Finding a balance between letting them see my pain and fear as a human being and letting them know that it isn't their responsibility to fix it for me gets more challenging the older they get and the closer I get to losing Mom. But I am determined to let them be children, to spend a few more years ensconced in the protective knowledge that they will be cared for, nurtured, and loved as they explore and become who they are. Maybe one day when they are adults and they have built their own solid foundations, if I need their help, they can come to my aid, but until then, I can't steal their adolescence by asking them to solve adult problems for which they aren't equipped.

I am incredibly grateful for Susan because of this. She was an adult in my life who never needed me to take care of her, and she was always willing to step in and mother me when I let her.

———

"Do they make noise when you walk?" Erin stands next to me in the shoe store. She and Lauren are my fashion experts. I never buy a pair of boots or a purse without consulting them first. I laugh out loud, not because it sounds like a ridiculous question, but because I completely understand what she means. In that instant, an image of them playing dress-up as toddlers fuzzes into my mind. Their arms filled with tulle and satin, they ferried outfits from the carpeted playroom to the hardwood floor of the kitchen, emptying the dress-up box trip by trip because that was where the plastic princess shoes made a really satisfying *clop, clop, clop.*

"Children should be seen and not heard," was a phrase often repeated in my childhood home, except it seemed as though the boys were somehow exempt. They were encouraged to roughhouse and wrestle, yelp wildly through a game of cowboys and Indians, holler affirmations and pump their fists in the air when they won a game of H-O-R-S-E. The girls were expected to sit quietly and color and if we made any sort of exuberant noise we were shushed posthaste.

Even before Mom and Dad divorced, I was well versed in the expectations of silent servitude. My job was to anticipate what needed to be done and do it without protest or inquiry. I learned that "chatterbox" was decidedly *not* a compliment, that challenging house rules, even in a calm voice, earned me a belt slash across the backside, and that my charm and value rose in direct proportion to how well I conformed and made peace between my siblings.

When Dad left and Mom went to work full-time, I was poised to become the one doing the shushing, reminding Katy to raise her hand in class if she had a question, perfecting the laser eye to still her lips at the dinner table, installing an inner monologue in her head designed to help her determine whether her input was important or necessary or just noise.

When Katy and I were molested, my brain took over and did the shushing without me asking. Automatically, instinctively, it must have known that it wouldn't do to upset the grown-ups. Mom had no choice but to pay this woman to watch us when she was at work. I knew she would rather be home with us and telling would only hurt her and make things worse for everyone. Instead of fighting, I began a months-long campaign to convince Mom that I was responsible enough to be in charge for a few hours after school until she got home. I didn't yell, scream, argue, or debate. I learned to cook and clean. I showed her how much better it would be to come home from work to a hot meal and happy kids than to make us stay at the babysitter's house.

My report cards reflected how strongly I embraced the notion that my best contributions came about when I listened instead of talked and did exactly what was expected of me. My teachers noted that I was a "team player" and "silent and attentive in class." I equated compliance with excellence.

After sending Erin to four years of Montessori school where she was encouraged to think independently and ask lots of questions, Sean and I decided it was time to enroll her in the local public elementary school. For weeks she came home agitated and upset, bored and frustrated. Most mornings, she begged me not to make her go back, but she couldn't articulate exactly why. Six weeks into the school year, we had our first parent-teacher conference. Sitting in small, plastic chairs across the desk from Erin's teacher, I noted that her desk was spotless. She appeared to be in her mid-50s, reading glasses hanging from a brass chain around her neck and a cardigan thrown on her shoulders. She looked like she could have been one of my elementary teachers in the 1970s.

"Erin is an exemplary student. She is quiet in class, pays attention, and turns her homework in on time. She doesn't ask questions or move around. She just does what I ask her to. I wish they were all like that."

Bile rose in my throat. This was an attempt to surgically remove my daughter's belief that she could be an active participant in her own life and replace it with the notion of quiet compliance. The last thing I wanted my daughters to believe was that their most valuable assets came in the form of shutting up and sitting still. I wanted them to question, explore, push beyond the boundaries, express their ideas and opinions without worrying whether they were different, and if being different meant they were wrong. I wanted them to find space for their voices and practice using them.

Susan taught me the power of my own voice. She was the one to whom I confessed my sordid little secrets. She was the one who took me to my first political rally. She was the first adult who made it a priority to listen to me instead of imploring me to be quiet. She helped me begin to see my own worth as something that came from inside me rather than something that was determined by other people.

It took me decades to break free of the idea that there were prescribed, acceptable ways for a young woman to make noise—on the basketball court or in a cheerful response to a man's question. I absorbed messages from my own family as well as the confusing cultural signals about when women are allowed to speak up (but *never* speak out), and how to appropriately show emotion without going overboard or risking labels like "hysterical" or "oversensitive." I learned which subjects were feminine. I can remember screaming into a pillow so that I wouldn't bother Mom if she was upset or sleeping. I weighed each syllable I spoke carefully on my tongue before I released it, assessing purpose and premise and potential fallout. Even when I knew something needed to be said, I forced my tongue to the roof of my mouth and took deep breaths because *it wasn't my place, I hadn't been invited, I shouldn't rock the boat.*

I swore I would raise my daughters differently.

Erin convinced me to buy the boots that made noise when I walk. She confessed that part of the reason she loves our house is because it has hardwood floors. She wears her heels all day long, walking purposefully from her room to her sister's room, to the bathroom and down the stairs for dinner. Sometimes when I am in the middle of cooking or working, I stop and look up and smile, listening to the rhythm and cadence of my daughter making noise. Lauren doesn't wear shoes in the house, but she plays her guitar and sings loudly, not caring if the neighbors hear. Dinnertime is a tumble of words and opinions and laughter and, sometimes, shouting. I am teaching my girls that the only thing they need to weigh when they open their mouths to speak is whether what they are about to say is kind, not whether they have any right to speak at all.

On the morning of the first day of school, after the girls had left the house, I put on my sneakers and went for a walk. Instead of going along the paved road, I veered off onto a gravel path and listened to the sound of my feet crunching in the still, cool morning air. I love the sound of shoes on a gravel path. It is my reminder: *I am here, I am here, I am here. I make noise, I have worth, I am here.* I walked and said a silent prayer for my daughters and myself. *May our words come clearly and easily. May we always remember to announce our presence with footsteps and sentences and laughter or outrage. May we always stand our ground and know our worth. We are here, we are here, we are here. We make noise. We have worth. We are here.*

Heart Openers

"My brain is just mush right now!"

"It's all just a blur. I don't know why I can't remember."

"You can put it in that . . . thing over there that is meant to have food in it. That big, white thing. Right there."

Mom is struggling, and while I sometimes spend time searching for the why—is it diabetes or her thyroid or some new medication or just the relentless march of Alzheimer's yet undiagnosed—ultimately it doesn't really matter. The reality is, she can't be alone these days without consequences, and since her husband, Ken, is heading back to the hospital for another round of surgery, Chris and I will have to tag-team taking care of her.

I get up at the crack of dawn on Saturday morning and head south on I-5. I drive for a little over four hours, chasing NPR stations without one pit stop to eat or pee. It's been six months since I saw her, although we talk on the phone every few days and I'm increasingly worried about her. She seems more and more confused every time we talk, but Ken insists she is just tired or stressed, or she forgot to eat. The fact is, I'm busy with work and teenage daughters, and it's easier to believe him than it is to push.

I'm not quite sure what I'll find when I get there, but I'm on edge. Ken has been in the hospital since Thursday morning and, ridiculously, Mom drove him there and sat vigil while he was in surgery, calling me every few hours to report. With each subsequent call, she sounded increasingly panicky and lost. By the fourth call, she had lost the thread that he was there for surgery, telling me that she couldn't understand why the doctors were giving him antibiotics and wouldn't let him come home. Even after he was in the recovery room and she was able to sit with him, he was too doped up to respond to her, so she kept calling me. I knew her blood sugar was likely dangerously low, but I couldn't get a straight answer out of her as to whether she had eaten all day or not.

By 7:30 that night, she called me to report that she was home after spending an hour searching for her car in the parking lot at their small, local hospital. I was simultaneously grateful that she was home in one piece and furious that she had driven at all. She sounded absolutely exhausted, but I encouraged her to go to the kitchen and make herself a peanut butter sandwich. I was terrified that she would turn the stove on and burn the house down, so I stayed on the line while she poured herself some juice, but she finally said she was too tired to eat and hung up. I called Susan, who lives a mile from her house, and begged her to go over and check on Mom. Chris wasn't able to come until Friday, and I was terrified that she would wake up without Ken there and freak out and try to leave again.

When I checked on her Friday morning, she wasn't sure whether she was going to visit Ken or not. She knew he was at the hospital, but said he was there for a "bad cold" and wanted him to come home. Chris spent Friday afternoon and evening with her and texted me updates that freaked us both out. He considered hiding her car keys but couldn't get her out of the room long enough to dig through her purse to find them.

When I arrive in Salem, Mom is at home, anxious to go visit Ken. More than once, during the ten-minute drive, she asks me where we are going and then remarks that she is glad I know how to get there, because she has no idea where we are. I shake my head, wondering how long it took her to find her way home from the hospital on Thursday night and thanking my lucky stars that she didn't get into an accident.

Over the next few days, we go visit Ken for a couple of hours and come straight home. I take her out to lunch once, but the activity in the restaurant stresses her out. She can't figure out why we're there or where this place is in relation to home. She tries really hard to hold on to the thread of the conversation and pay attention to what I'm saying, but it is clearly exhausting. I am reminded of what it was like to be in France last summer. I know enough French to get my basic needs met, and I can read it okay, but when I was surrounded by native speakers talking at their normal rate (which seems inordinately fast), it was physically taxing to spend an entire day paying close enough attention to pick out the salient details I needed to navigate the city. I wonder if that's how Mom feels—like there is some familiarity of language, but it keeps slipping away from her and she has to keep redirecting her focus to try and understand.

At home, I can't just sit with her, so I busy myself making chicken enchiladas and chili and meatloaf that I can portion out and put in the freezer so that Ken doesn't have to cook for a while during his recovery. Every once in a while, she gets up from the couch and pokes her head in to the kitchen and asks, "What'cha doin'?"

"Cooking, Mom. You love cooking. Want to help?"

"Nope." Her eyes cloud over, and I think she must be trying to figure out if she really does love cooking.

I am reminded of what it's like to have a toddler. I am on constant alert, watching for her to leave the room, trying to find activities that she might enjoy, cajoling her to take her medications. She is particularly resistant to the latter. When I get up in the morning and pour our coffee, I reach up to grab the pill container Ken has stocked for the week he is away and tip her pills into my hand. When I offer them to her, her eyes narrow.

"You're just like Ken. Trying to control me. I don't need your help. I will take those when I want to."

"Let's just take them now, Mom. I'll take mine, too." I show her my own pill container, stocked with the vitamins and hormones I've found that keep my depression and anxiety at bay. "If we both take them together, then we don't have to worry about whether or not we took them, later."

She takes the handful of pills from me and places them gently on the counter in front of her. She won't make eye contact, and I sense that she is being cagey.

"Do we have anything for breakfast?" she asks me just as the toast pops up from the toaster. I turn to take it out and see her swipe the pills into the pocket of her robe out of the corner of my eye. She is sneaky. She never did like to be bossed around. While I know I need to somehow get her to take the pills, I also suppress a smile, quietly celebrating the fact that she is still willing to assert herself in some way.

I am operating on obligation and love and guilt. As resentful as I was about having to do this kind of thing for Mom, the irony of it is that I am frustrated that I live so far away and can't do more. The thing about me structuring my life and my identity around taking care of people is that I always have to have someone in my life who needs to be taken care of if I'm going to stay relevant. But Ken seems to think that they're doing just fine and, other than times like this when he physically can't be here, he isn't looking for my help or my input. They have been married for over twenty years, but I still have this odd sense of ownership when it comes to Mom. I've offered to accompany them to doctor's appointments, pay for nursing care, and research insurance benefits and other care options, and he has politely refused each of those things. He's got this. So, for now, this is my only gig. And I'm torn between feeling dismissed and feeling relieved. Because, the fact is, this gig is exhausting.

I keep telling the same stories over and over again, hoping to set them in her brain somewhere, but sometimes when I talk, I can see her eyes just go dim. She isn't paying attention. It's too much work. I follow her everywhere, remembering my grandmother's tendency to simply sneak out of the house and wander off, but she doesn't like me acting as her shadow. I'm afraid to go pee because I don't want to lose sight of her, and even when I console myself with the fact that I'd hear the front door open and be able to catch up with her, I'm still not sure what I'd say to get her back inside without a fight.

I am throwing a load of laundry in the dryer when I hear her turning the doorknob on the guest room frantically.

"Hey, where's the key for this room? Why did Ken lock this? I need to get in here."

I poke my head out and look at her. What? The guest room door is locked?

"I don't know, Mom. I didn't even know it was locked. We can ask Ken when we go visit him today. What do you need?"

"I need Ken to stop playing games! He is trying to control me!" Her eyes are brimming with tears and her hand rattles the doorknob. "I need to get in here! Why would he lock me out of a room in my own house? Isn't this my house?" The last question comes as a genuine curiosity. Shit. She isn't even sure this is her house.

I put my hand on her shoulder and lead her in to the family room and settle her on the couch. She is agitated and her eyes are wild. I'm not sure if she is angry or confused or what, but I feel like crying. And then, her cat, Moses, shows up.

My mother loves animals, but none more than cats. There has not been a day in my life that she has not lived with at least one cat, although I've never known her to seek one out. Somehow, the strays always manage to find her and move in.

My grandmother hated cats. I don't know precisely why, but despite the fact that almost all five of her children grew up to have cats for pets, she was disdainful of them and wanted nothing to do with them. Grandma loved baseball, teaching, reading, and traveling. Cats, she had no time or love for. Until she developed Alzheimer's.

My aunt and uncle had a house in the hills above Santa Barbara and one summer, shortly after my grandmother began really struggling with her memory, a wildfire ripped through those hills and burned their house to the ground. For an agonizing few days, the family looked for their beloved cat, Cecil. When they found him, hiding among the hills, safe and sound, Grandma fell in love with him. We were all astonished. This woman who, for sixty years or more, had loudly proclaimed her hatred for felines, suddenly found a companion in Cecil, an enormous orange and white tabby.

Moses showed up as one of a litter of cats that a stray delivered in the crawl space beneath Mom and Ken's house. Years ago, Sean and I brought Erin and Lauren to visit during the summer and while we were having a barbecue in the backyard, we heard a chorus of pitiful wailing. Mom said that there were at least three kittens living underneath their house, and they were starving. She had tried to fish them out, but couldn't, and their mother had either abandoned them for good, or was out trying to find food for them.

Never one to back down from a challenge, I asked her to point out where she saw them and I went to work. Armed with a can of tuna and a length of yarn, I lay on my belly on the concrete patio and slowly coaxed each kitten close enough to me to grab it by the scruff of the neck, one by one. Within 20 minutes, I had gotten all four mangy, skinny, starving kittens out from beneath the house.

Mom and Ken found homes for three of the kittens and kept Moses, and he is the biggest damn cat I've ever seen. He must weigh 40 pounds, and part of that is because Mom feeds him over and over again all day long, forgetting that she has already done it, and he isn't about to protest.

During the day, as I putter around the house doing laundry and cooking and cleaning the bathroom, Mom looks for him. She asks over and over again, "Where is that Moses? Where could he be?" She walks from room to room in their tiny house, searching for him. When she finds him and settles down on the couch with him, it is transformative.

Her face relaxes, her shoulders relax, her entire being settles. I don't know if it is the tactile experience of petting him or his rhythmic purring, the weight (oh, the weight!) on her lap, or just the fact that she can communicate nonverbally, but she is at ease. She can just interact with him by sitting quietly and petting him, and there is no expectation that she will remember or make conversation.

It's no wonder she looks for him all day long. He is familiar to her and she can do exactly the things he expects of her—feed him, let him in and out of the house, and sit with him quietly. It must be a huge relief to get moments during the day that are like this when so much else feels confusing and chaotic.

I wonder whether I can find a way to do this for her, too. It reminds me of sitting with Daddy on his last day, just being.

––––––––––

On the way home, a hurricane of emotions picks me up and throws me back and forth. I agonize over the four-hour distance between us, the kids I have at home that still need me around a lot, thoughts of what might lie ahead. I rail at the genetic sequence that puts this destination squarely within my own sights—both of my grandmothers had early-onset Alzheimer's disease and now my mother does, too—and I call Sean from the road to remind him that he has orders to push me off the edge of the Grand Canyon as soon as I forget the names of close friends and family. Time and time again, I am mentally sucked back into the ruts that demand I "fix it," find a solution, put some plan in place that makes sense.

I am beginning to understand that when I feel the need to seek out something I can take care of, it is probably because I have something I want to avoid in my own life. It is far easier to solve someone else's problems than it is to look at my own. Throughout my life, I've spent hours—days, even—contemplating possible solutions to a loved one's predicament. I have contacted people in my social network, offered names and ideas, baked bread and casseroles, babysat kids, and driven miles out of my way to ease someone's pain or make their life easier or take something off their plate. And while those things are often genuinely helpful, when I start to exaggerate the importance of doing those things, make offers to help when I haven't been asked, and look for people who are hurting, it is a sign that there is something wrong in my life. When I am feeling stuck or sad, I sometimes cast about for others who are struggling in order to distract me from my own issues and to make myself feel competent. I pat myself on the back for my ability to fix things, smooth things over, clear a path, see a situation from the ten-thousand-foot view, where things seem so much clearer than they do when I'm sitting in my own muck with no perspective at all.

At some point, I hear a voice reminding me that this isn't about me and the swirl of thoughts settles. This is about Mom. During the last several days with her, I saw glimpses of fear in her eyes, and it cracked me open. What does she know about what she is losing?

I think about how fear motivates us, forces us to push away, and shrinks us. I think about how it makes us defensive and reactionary, even if we try to trick ourselves into thinking that we're going on the offensive. As a mother to my sister and my daughters, fear made me work to avoid or prevent the things I didn't want to see happen. I was so often in protection mode, and I wonder how that impacted the way I showed up for the people I love the most. How often did I choose flight or fight instead of love and hope?

I decide that hope is the force that propels us forward. It opens up creativity and channels of positivity that help us define what we want. Hope is proactive and deals in reality. Fear is reactive and trades in extremes, and as a kid, I saw my parents mostly live in the realm of fear, either because they did or because my brain was primed to recognize fear over hope. As I took on the role of parent as a young person, I was caring for myself as much as I was caring for my sister and I carried that over into the way I parent my daughters. It was only when I began to fall apart under the strain of living in fear that I learned to embrace possibility and hope and the power of gratitude.

There were so many moments during the last several days when I felt a sense of gratitude and affection from Mom as she watched me cook and drive her to visit Ken and sit with her and Moses. I am beginning to understand that the real work of healing myself will happen in the context of this relationship and the relationships I have with Katy and Erin and Lauren. When I lead with love and work to be present, I can begin to heal my own inner child and, in this way, I see the act of taking care of others as a way of taking care of myself. And at this point, the only thing I can do with Mom is simply show up and love her. I crank up the music and sing.

Evolution

"Moooooo-ooooom, will you untangle my necklace for me? I need to wear it today." Erin thrusts a silver mess in to my hands and whirls into the bathroom to dry her hair.

Rather than being annoyed at this task, I am pleased. I am good at this. It's one of the odd things I can do with ease. Slowly and methodically pulling the links through each other to loosen the knots is Zen-like. Even as a kid who had a hard time sitting still, this was one thing I excelled at. Using my long fingernails to gently tease the strands loose from each other, I wonder if this is something Erin and Lauren will remember one day—my odd ability to undo knots in necklaces and bracelets.

What do I remember Mom for? Two things instantly come into focus in my mind—her chili and lasagna.

I feel guilty. I should be able to think of something more than that.

I call Mom every few days to check in and she is always thrilled to hear from me. At this point, she still recognizes my voice—although she is sometimes sure I am her sister, Kari (she doesn't have a sister named Kari)—and I am grateful. Today when I call, I am struggling with an issue at work and I ask her if I can vent.

"Sure! Tell me what's happening." She perks up, and I suddenly remember the part of her life where she sold real estate for thirty years.

As I rant about the situation I find myself in with a business partner who is trying to convince me to do something I'm not comfortable with, something magical happens. Mom makes all the right noises in all the right places. When I lament that I think the entire deal will soon crumble, I recall all the sales Mom worked on for weeks at a time that fell apart for one reason or another.

"How did you handle that? Did it make you crazy to work so hard for so long on something and have the other agent just screech to a halt or sabotage the deal? It must have been so hard!"

"Hmmm, I suppose it must have been. I don't remember. But you stick to your guns, Kari. You can't let this deal happen if you don't feel good about it. You deserve to have it happen just the way you want it to. Don't let him bully you."

"Thanks, Mom. It is frustrating, but you're right. I have to hold firm boundaries. Thanks for letting me dominate the conversation and vent."

"Oh, honey, thank you! You just made my day, calling to talk to me. Call and vent anytime. I love hearing from you!"

We hang up, and I am struck by the changes Mom has gone through. For most of my life, she was a card-carrying expert in Catholic guilt who could sling a backhanded compliment like nobody's business. More times than I care to count, I have been on the receiving end of something that, on paper, looked like a proud-mama observation, but in real life, delivered in a sarcastic tone, was actually a biting commentary on my life or my personality. But in the last year, she has become increasingly gracious and grateful. Over the past two decades, our rare phone conversations all ended with her saying, "Okay, then." These days, she does everything she can to extend our phone calls and always remarks on how happy she is to hear from me. She ends every conversation with "I love you" and asks when I can come visit her again.

All of this has prompted a change in me, too. I genuinely hope that she has been released from all the memories she doesn't want to have. For so many years I longed to take her by the hand and lead her to the stinking pile of misery I had so carefully catalogued. I wanted to present her with incontrovertible evidence of the times when I needed her, and she pretended not to notice or turned it around to prove that she needed me more. I wanted to show her something that would make her admit to me that I wasn't crazy, that things were actually as bad as I thought they were.

What I know now is that that pile is mine and not hers. And if she has a pile, I hope that it has been swept away from her mind just like the name of her favorite restaurant or the company she used to work for. I hope that her thoughts these days are peaceful and amused and that she isn't beating herself up for things she did or didn't do.

––––––––––

The last time I visited, Ken asked me to take Mom to the Saturday market to buy some tomato plants for their patio. We walked through the throngs of shoppers on a sunny day, listening to music and eating at food trucks, and I watched her carefully for signs of agitation. She doesn't venture out often and gets overwhelmed easily by crowds and noises and unfamiliar places.

After choosing the tomato plants, I asked her if she wanted some flowers to plant out back, too, and she said yes. We walked toward the nursery vendor's table, and I smelled the marigolds before I saw them. Every spring when I was growing up, Mom bought flats of yellow and orange marigolds to plant along the driveway in Klamath Falls. We alternated the colors in a pattern, and they stood up like little soldiers, flanking the shiny cars we washed and waxed every sunny weekend day. I recoiled as the scent of marigolds conjured up painful memories of me sitting on the front stoop picking at the peeling grey paint with my shoes. To the left, in my memory, I could see the pink flowers of the crabapple tree I used to hide in and to the right, the orderly line of orange-yellow-orange-yellow-orange-yellow marigolds, the Holt Adoption van backing out of the driveway with Cameron's face framed in the window, one hand on the glass. I wasn't sure I could keep walking toward the flower display.

The top shelf of the flower seller's cart was packed with the petite purple faces of violas, streaked through with darker purple. The blossoms bounced lightly in the breeze. Mom stopped, confused, and asked why we were there. I reminded her that she wanted some flowers to plant in the backyard, and she nodded eagerly. I pointed to the violas with their cheery faces, but she bent down to choose a flat of marigolds.

I wonder if she chose them because somewhere in her mind she remembers planting them somewhere else, or if it's just because she likes their bright colors better than the darker purple violas. Maybe she grabbed them because they were in a full flat, and she was in a hurry to get out of there and get home. I couldn't ask her why because she wouldn't understand the question, so I resigned myself to rolling the window down and breathing through my mouth on the way home. The smell still makes me physically ill.

I begin to realize that taking care of someone doesn't have anything to do with my idea of what is best. All the years I worked to take care of Mom and protect her feelings, what I was really doing was taking care of myself. With Katy, I was desperate to keep her from feeling any pain or acting in a way that would get her sent away—again, self-protection. I take care of my daughters to keep them safe, to turn them into what I think a good human being is and to show my love for them as though it will somehow reflect on me. There has always been some sort of ego boost I get from making things neat and tidy, satisfying the essentials, checking off the boxes. And it gives me a sense of control and predictability in my life.

But that isn't truly what taking care of others is all about. It is much more profound and impactful for me to set aside my values and assumptions and just love Mom and Katy and the girls and meet them where they are. It is harder, to be sure. It is more nebulous and far less predictable, and there is always a chance I will be asked to do something I don't want to do, but there is also a grace and a freedom in it. It allows me to let down my guard and just listen and hold space. It both makes me feel less frantic and responsible for them and more connected and affectionate. If I am not responsible for fixing anything, I am not worried about falling short of anyone's expectations.

As Mom's memories peel away, I begin to have space for other memories. Beyond the stories I've told myself over the years about who she is, and the episodes I've highlighted that support that narrative, there is so much more. As I sit down to design eighth-grade graduation cards for Lauren and her closest girlfriends, I pick up a calligraphy pen and realize that it was Mom that taught me to do this. I remember her fastidious attention to lining the letters up on the page, making sure that the entire message fit before she put the nib to the parchment. She was recruited to fill the names in on certificates of all kinds when I was a kid because her calligraphy skills were so beautiful. I remember excursions to Crater Lake after Dad left when she taught us to cross-country ski. My image of her is expanding as she and I both shed old ways of relating along with her short-term memory.

My mind is wired to look for danger, to find gaps and errors. The challenges I faced as a kid created superhighways in my brain that taught me that the world was a scary place and I had to be on guard all the time. Those superhighways carry me from observation to expectation of disaster with no off-ramps, but if I'm going to make room for happiness, I have to start finding alternate routes.

I resolve to start looking for the things that are good and right in my world, paying attention to people treating others with kindness and compassion, exploring possibilities for peace and connection and really appreciating them. In the beginning it feels trite and Pollyanna-ish, but I have to keep trying if I'm going to make it work.

I also begin looking for examples in my own life where people cared for me in a way that was meaningful and profound because I'm pretty sure that most of my life, my idea of "taking care" of someone was a bit off the mark. Susan is the first person who comes to mind. She never tried to change me or pretend that what I was going through as a kid wasn't hard. She encouraged me and listened to me, and I knew she was always there when I needed her.

When Dad and I reconciled, he became that kind of person in my life, too. He was loving and supportive and never minimized my feelings or tried to get me to hide them because he couldn't handle seeing me struggle.

As I get older, I seek out friends who will do that for me—listen and acknowledge my right to have whatever perspective I have without trying to change it or fix it. People who can stand to watch me in pain without shying away or needing to get busy doing something are rare and precious. People who don't rush to explain away my sadness or counter it with a story they think is more agonizing are hard to find, but I know that is the stuff true compassion and empathy are made of, and cultivating those relationships is essential for my mental health.

Creating Space

The dog, CB, has been more and more off lately, and I know I shouldn't be surprised. He is twelve, but he has always been my rock. He is my companion when I call Mom, and he is my excuse to get away from my computer when I simply can't sit still any longer. He reads my moods and comes to sit at my feet when I'm sad or frustrated, and he makes me laugh with his insistent prodding when he thinks it's time to play.

But these days, our walks are almost entirely full of intense, obsessive sniffing. He keeps his head down, doesn't prance around or roll in the grass, and sometimes he just stops in his tracks and refuses to walk any farther after half a block. He stands still for minutes at a time as though he's not sure where he is or what he is supposed to be doing. I don't have many options at that point other than to tug on him and encourage him forward, but I feel bad yanking on him constantly.

Today, it occurs to me that I don't really have anywhere else to be for a while, so I decide to let him be in charge even if it means stopping to sniff things for five minutes every few feet. He just keeps leading us farther and farther away from home and I start to worry about how we're going to get back, but he is much more relaxed and happy with this scenario than he is with me forcing the agenda, so I just keep following him.

That afternoon as I tell the vet about the times when CB starts shaking uncontrollably and panting like he has just run a marathon, his eyes wild, the vet breaks in and nods, "It's dementia."

I nearly laugh out loud. The irony.

"But the shaking and panting? He gets this look in his eyes that is just frantic and sometimes he tries to crawl in to my lap and wants to be held. It looks like a panic attack. That's dementia?"

"Dementia often triggers anxiety," he shrugs.

————————

The day has gotten away from me. I meant to call Mom this morning because she is always more confused in the afternoon, but I have to call now. It has been nearly a week since I checked in. I snap the leash on CB and head out with my phone.

"Hello?" She always answers the phone on the first ring.

"Hey, Mom, it's Kari. How are you?" I always announce myself in case she doesn't recognize my voice anymore.

"I'm fine." She is a little cautious. I'm not sure she knows who I am, but she's playing along anyway.

"So, what's up? Anything new with you?"

"That's exactly what Ken wants to know. He just got home from work and caught me lying on the bed in our room. I have a nasty headache and I was trying to get rid of it by taking a . . . you know . . . whatever you want to call it."

"A nap?"

"Is that what you call it when you're trying to get rid of a headache?"

"Well, yeah. Unless you mean taking an Advil."

"I *know* what an Advil is, thankyouverymuch."

Ooh, sarcasm. That's good. She's still in there somewhere.

"But the other thing. When you lay down."

"A nap. That's what I call it. I should let you go so you can go back and lie down."

She sighs. "No, it's fine. You called. And the cat just came and jumped on me so I don't think I'll be taking a . . . not-Advil-but-the-other-thing right now."

I feel like I'm in an Abbot and Costello routine.

"Are you sure? You can just push the cat off you and go to sleep." There's no way she could sleep with Moses on her—she would suffocate under his weight. I'm having trouble believing he jumped up on to the bed by himself. He looks like Jabba the Hutt with fur.

"No, I can't push the cat off. That would be mean. And Ken is home and you are on the phone. Maybe I don't need a whateveryoucallit."

"A nap. Did you take any Advil?"

"I know what Advil is. I wasn't taking one when you called. I was taking the other thing, or trying to."

"I know, Mom." I'm nearly in hysterics. The dog has taken a dump on the neighbor's lawn, and he is using all of his seventy pounds to try and drag me onward while I squat with a plastic bag on my hand and try to clean it up, my flat phone tucked precariously between my shoulder and ear.

"But sometimes taking Advil and a nap makes my headache go away," I say.

"Your headache? Do you have a headache? You sound like you're outside. You should go in. Is it bright out? That can make it worse."

Oh, God. I have the giggles.

"No, Mom. I don't have a headache. You do."

"I *know* that. I'd have to be nuts to not know that I have a headache!"

"Okay, I'm sorry. I was just trying to be helpful."

"By having a headache with me? That's crazy!"

I want her to be teasing me, but she isn't. She is absolutely genuine in her confusion. Strangely, instead of freaking me out, it's cracking me up.

"Never mind. Tell me what you've been doing lately."

"Trying to lie down and get rid of this headache."

"All right. I'll let you go then. You go lie down. I'll call you tomorrow. But maybe take an Advil before you nap."

"What is it with you and the Advil? Why are you so pushy? I just wanted to lie down and do that other thing we talked about."

"Okay. You do that. I'll call you tomorrow."

She heaves a huge sigh. "Okay. That sounds good. The next day."

"I love you."

In the last two decades, I have been called "Mom" by many of my daughters' friends and classmates. I have driven hours of carpool and chaperoned camping trips and excursions to museums and hikes. I have baked and hosted and cleaned up after parties and sat at the kitchen table engaged in difficult conversations with more than one of their friends. I have grinned to myself when I hear the sound of raucous laughter coming from the bedrooms upstairs or an impromptu dance party in the basement. I have almost never turned down a last-minute plea to let someone's friend sleep over because the truth is, there are few things I love more than knowing that I have created a safe space for these kids. I don't do it for pats on the back or so that I can be a martyr. I do it because I love it. It fills me up. That is why I took care of Dad when he was dying, because I could hold space for him to just be, exactly as he was, and it was one of the most gratifying experiences of my life. This, I know now, is the difference between taking care of someone because you have to and taking care of someone because you want to.

When I turn that corner in my mind with Mom, something amazing happens. I am able to meet her exactly where she is and as the layers of memories peel away from her mind, she becomes more present. Our weekly phone conversations are less about comparing what I wanted from her to what I thought I had gotten and more about camaraderie and compassion. When I offer Mom the kind of caretaking I have learned to offer others—simple love with no strings attached—I open myself up to receiving the kind of mothering I have always wanted, too. All it took was redefining what it meant to take care of someone. I suddenly have a much deeper understanding of another Pema Chödrön passage:

> Compassion is not a relationship between the healer and the wounded. It's a relationship between equals. Only when we know our own darkness well can we be present with the darkness of others. Compassion becomes real when we recognize our shared humanity.

I thought that since I had already lost one parent, there would be a sense of familiarity, of déjà vu, of been there-done-that as Mom continued to fail. Not in a dismissive way, but an "Okay, I've got this—I know what to expect" kind of way. But this experience is so different. Dad and I maintained our relationship on equal footing. We knew he was sick and we talked about it. Up until the tumor in his throat stole his voice, we spoke to each other every few days, and he knew who I was even as he died in my arms.

I have no road map for what's happening with Mom. She isn't having some diseased cells cut away or calling me to tell me about the latest drugs or therapies she's considering. She might live six months or six years. She has no idea who I am most of the time. This one-sided relationship is teeth-grindingly painful in a totally unique way because Mom's slide has been gradual except when it seems to leap forward. There have been times in the last year where she has almost been able to snap out of it and recognize me and have a short conversation, and that gives me hope and makes me want to figure out how to capture those lucid moments and multiply them. It is not unlike that jolt of adrenaline a gambler gets when the screen comes up three cherries after twenty losses in a row. It's just enough to keep you going until the next jackpot.

But those moments come less and less often, and I know I won't get any sort of signal that tells me I've seen the last one. There was no alarm bell that told me the last time we talked on the phone was the last time we would ever talk on the phone. I didn't get a warning when she called me by name for the final time, when she truly understood that I was her daughter, so that I could savor it or mark it somehow. Or brace myself for the fact that it won't happen ever again.

———

In November, I get a frantic email from Ken telling me that I need to come down. Mom hasn't slept for three days, and she doesn't know who he is. He can't do this anymore. By the time I make arrangements to come—ensuring that Erin and Lauren will be taken care of and asking Susan if I can bunk in her guest room—the crisis has passed. She has turned some corner and is back to where she was before. I decide to come anyway, if only to help Ken research assisted-living facilities and arrange finances and give him some respite.

She spends the majority of her time in bed. Ken says she sleeps eighteen hours a day, and he has her on a strict schedule so that he can get enough calories in to her to keep her blood sugar up. It takes her hours to finish a glass of water because she keeps forgetting it's there. She has to be prompted to take a bite of her sandwich every few minutes and every time, she looks down at her plate in surprise, as though she had no idea she had a sandwich. She is happy to have me there, but she can't track the conversation and she doesn't know my name. When Ken and I start talking to each other, she alternates between watching us like a tennis match and staring off into space. Her toenails and fingernails are so long they are starting to curl in on themselves, but Ken gets her up and dressed every day and helps her put makeup on. He does all the laundry and shopping and cooking and takes such tender care of her.

I ask her about the cat, and she gives me a blank look. What cat? She doesn't have a cat. By the end of our visit, I'm not convinced she knows who Ken is anymore, either, but she does know he is her caretaker. I head back to Susan's and sit in her living room and cry. Some major shift has happened, and it's clear there will be no more lucid moments. My mother doesn't know who I am.

I think about why that is so hard. Part of me says just get on with loving her the best way I know how without worrying whether she remembers that I am hers, but another part of me screams to be special. I don't want to be just one of the cast of characters who comes through to visit and smile at her. I want to be her daughter. There is something about the reciprocity of a loving relationship that makes it feel whole.

As I sat with Dad during his last few days, holding his hand and telling him stories, even though he couldn't speak, there was a familiarity. He squeezed my hand and his eyes danced when I said something funny. His rough, calloused thumb rubbed back and forth against mine when I was being serious. We had a history that was fully intact until the moment he took his last breath and when I grieved for him, I grieved for all of him—his body, his Self, and our relationship.

This time, I am grieving in stages. The last time I was with Mom, I saw a flash of her old self shine through when she made a snarky comment to Ken. But we have lost our shared history. Our inside jokes now belong to me alone and when I sit with her, I can't tell her stories about Erin or Lauren because she doesn't know who they are and that confuses her. We can't reminisce or look forward together. There is a quality of suspended animation, a sense that I am walking without a foundation.

Perspective

I fixed the saltcellar this morning. It wasn't terribly complicated, but it took a little bit of ingenuity and some focus and a real desire to have it fixed. I made it last year at one of those paint-your-own-ceramics work-shops. Erin and I were having a mom-and-daughter day and I decided the last thing our cupboards needed was another coffee mug, so I chose this ceramic salt container with a rubber flange on the lid to keep it airtight and Erin pronounced it "cute," which is an enormous compliment coming from a sixteen-year-old girl who is your daughter.

It lasted about a week before the wooden lid came loose from the part with the rubber seal, and Lauren decided to shove it farther down inside rather than trying to pry it loose. This resulted in the container being full of salt beneath part of the lid that was firmly stuck halfway down, and no way to remove it. We left it like that for months, filling the upper part of the container with salt and calling it good.

But this morning as I stood over a pan of hash browns, imagining what it is going to be like to pack Mom's stuff up and move her to memory care in the next week or so, I took on a project I thought I could fix. As tears tracked slowly down my cheeks, I contemplated what it would take to pry the lid out. I started by running a sharp knife around the edge of the rubber, hoping to ease it loose, but abandoned that after imagining the knife slipping out and slicing my finger. Next, I got a corkscrew and tried to drive it into the center of the wood to get ahold of it and lift up, but the wood was too dense. When I went to the junk drawer to get a screwdriver and screw, I heard Dad's voice in my head, telling me this was the ticket.

I screwed it in until it just took hold and then grabbed the vise grips, stopping for a second to wonder how many other households have a pair of vise grips in the kitchen drawer and mentally patting myself on the back for my cleverness. I clamped them over the top of the screw and gently rocked the vise grips back and forth until the lid slid up and out.

I flipped Erin's hash browns to crisp up on the other side, put the tools away, and grabbed the superglue. Within minutes, the potatoes were on a plate and the two halves of the lid were tightly bonded back together. I washed out the saltcellar, refilled it with fresh salt, and wiped down the counter.

When Erin came in to eat, she opened it up, pinched out a bit of salt, and sprinkled it on her potatoes. She didn't even notice that it was fixed. Part of me was offended, and the other part of me felt as though this is what I want for my daughters for the next little while—to know that if there are things in their world that can be set right, they can just assume that I will make it happen.

───────

When I was in college, one of my philosophy professors explained his theory of personal evolution as an ever-widening spiral. He said he envisions us being born, starting at a fixed point at the bottom, and as we grow and learn, we make our way up and around, which is why we often feel like we are back in the same place we were before, over and over again, repeating patterns. But, he said, if we are really paying attention, we begin to notice that as we circle back around, each time we are one plane higher than before with a more complete view. In this way, we continue to build on our own experiences, widening the spiral and climbing higher and higher, expanding our understanding with the ability to look back and see how far we've come.

When Erin and Lauren were toddlers, Mom and Ken and Sean and I took them to the Oregon State Fair. We rode a few carnival rides, ate elephant ears and funnel cakes, and had their faces painted with fairies and rainbows. In the hottest part of the day, when the girls were exhausted, Erin rode in the stroller and Sean carried Lauren as we wandered through the craft booths. When we came upon a booth selling yard ornaments made of thick metal rods twisted in to spirals, I remembered my professor. The brightly-colored figures hung from the tent ceiling, each with a large marble resting in one of the lower spirals. When you rotated it from the bottom, an optical illusion made it seem as though the marble was falling lower and lower. Erin and Lauren squealed with delight and begged us to turn one and then another and another. They giggled and worried that the marble would fall out and crash to the floor, and Erin struggled to get out of the stroller to cup her hands beneath one of them just in case it fell. I told her it wouldn't fall, but she didn't believe me. Sean and I were so amused by their reaction that we bought one to take home.

Listening to the professor's lecture, I drew spiral after spiral in my notebook, letting my mind wander and promising that I'd never find myself back where I had been before. Back then, I preferred to think of myself as a shooting star, hurtling light years away from my rocky beginnings, never to return. But these days, that spiral is incredibly satisfying. It hangs outside the kitchen window where I can see it when I wash dishes. The girls no longer even notice it, but I love being reminded that even when it feels like I'm right back where I was before, I'm not. I'm older and stronger and wiser, and I know better what it means to take care of the people you love and yourself in ways that are truly meaningful.

Acknowledgments

I have so much gratitude for so many people, I'm not even sure where to begin. But I guess, if I'm starting at the most logical point, I have to say thank you to my family. Thank you, Mom and Dad, for creating the family you did, for Chris and Katy and Cameron. Chris, thank you for being the best big brother a person could hope for—irreverent, kind, unabashedly yourself. Katy, thank you for letting me hold you, for teaching me what it is to love someone unconditionally even when they're not your blood relative. Thank you for being my sister. Erin and Lauren, thank you for loving me as I am and calling me Mom. You teach me something amazing every day, and it is an absolute honor to witness the way you move through the world. Alex and Moses and SJ, Midori and Nia and Maia, thanks for being my "extra" kids and showing me what a joy it is to be surrounded by strong young women who can do anything they want to. Susan, thank you for your steadfast support and for helping me find my voice and use it.

Thank you to the amazing women writers who have supported, encouraged, and nurtured my work throughout the last decade. Hope Edelman, your book *Motherless Daughters* started it all. Jennifer Lauck, I hated it at the time, but thank you for pushing me to write about the things I least wanted to write. Carrie Wilson Link, Michelle O'Neal, Jess Byers, Holly Goodman, Emily Hine, Lisa Romeo, Judy Ryan Hall, Monica Holloway, Kim Wyatt, Tanya Ward Goodman, Elizabeth Aquino, and Claire Dederer: you have all read portions of this work and helped me shape it in to something I love and am proud of. I am so grateful for your time and wisdom and expertise. Binders, you are exceptional and a vast source of all that is good in the world.

Jodie Levy, Tracy Piette, Becky Tilles, and Thereza Howling, you are a girl's best friends. Thank you for the love and laughter and never-ending support for my family and me. You are my chosen family, and I can't imagine a better one out there.

To my crazy Ukrainian clan: I am so pleased to be part of your antics and to have my daughters fully embraced by the warmth and love you all exude. Here's to many more adventures.

Last but not least, thank you to Joan Cusack Handler for taking a chance on this book and this writer. Thank you to Gabriel and Joy and Baron and Ryan for reading this story over and over again and helping me make it the best it can be. I was over the moon at the chance to work with you all as we brought this book to the world.

CavanKerry's Mission

CavanKerry is committed to expanding the reach of poetry and other fine literature to a general readership by publishing works that explore the emotional and psychological landscapes of everyday life and relationships.

Other Books in the Memoir Series

Confessions of Joan the Tall, Joan Cusack Handler
Primary Lessons, Sarah Bracey White
My Mother's Funeral, Adriana Páramo

Truth Has a Different Shape has been set in Arno Pro, which was created by Robert Slimbach at Adobe. The name refers to the river that runs through Florence, Italy.